WORDS
and
WORLDS.

ALSO BY ALISON LURIE

Fiction
Love and Friendship
The Nowhere City
Imaginary Friends
Real People
The War Between the Tates
Only Children
Foreign Affairs
The Truth About Lorin Jones
Women and Ghosts
The Last Resort
Truth and Consequences

Nonfiction
The Language of Clothes
Don't Tell the Grown-ups
Boys and Girls Forever
Familiar Spirits
The Language of Houses
Reading for Fun

WORDS *and* WORLDS

FROM AUTOBIOGRAPHY

TO ZIPPERS

ALISON LURIE

DELPHINIUM BOOKS

WORDS AND WORLDS

For information, address DELPHINIUM BOOKS, INC.,

16350 Ventura Boulevard, Suite D

PO Box 803

Encino, CA 91436

The essays in this book originally appeared in slightly different form: "Nobody
Asked You to Write a Novel" and "Zippers" in the *New York Times Book
Review*; "Their Harvard" in *My Harvard, My Yale* (Harvard University Press),
"Life After Fashion" and "Breaking the Laws of Fashion" in *The Guardian*;
"What Happened in Hamlet" in *The New Review* (London); "The Language
of Deconstruction," "Witches," "Barbara Epstein," "Edward Gorey," "James
Merrill," "The Good Bad Boy: Pinocchio," "The Royal Family of Elephants,"
"Saying No to Narnia," "Harry Potter Revisited," and "Rapunzel: The Girl
in the Tower" in the *New York Review of Books*; "My Name or Yours?" in
the *Observer* (London); "A. R. Ammons" in *The Bookpress* (Ithaca, NY); "Bad
Husbands" in *American Scholar*; "The Dark Side of Knitting" in *The New Yorker*

Library of Congress Cataloguing-in-Publication Data is available on request.

ISBN 978-1-88-328578-4

19 20 21 22 23 LSC 10 9 8 7 6 5 4 3 2 1

First Edition

Jacket and interior design by Greg Mortimer

For Edward Hower

Contents

PREFACE   3

PERSONAL HISTORY
Nobody Asked You to Write a Novel   7
Their Harvard   16

WORDS AND WORLDS
What Happened in *Hamlet*   31
The Language of Deconstruction   61
My Name or Yours   70
Witches Old and New   75

PEOPLE
Archie's Gifts   97
Barbara Epstein   100
Edward Gorey   105
James Merrill   116

CHILDREN'S BOOKS
The Good Bad Boy: Pinocchio   121
The Royal Family of Elephants   135
Saying No to Narnia   154
Harry Potter Revisited   172
Bad Husbands   184
Rapunzel: The Girl in the Tower   189

CLOTHES

Breaking the Laws of Fashion   205
Aprons   210
The Mystery of Knitting   215
Zippers   224
Life After Fashion   227

Preface

Over the years many people have told me that they want to be a writer. It gradually becomes clear what some of them have in mind: they are daydreaming of becoming a special sort of person who will be recognized as more sensitive and creative than others, with a more interesting personality. If they ask me about agents and publishers and reviewers, I know that they are also daydreaming of fame and fortune: of articles and photographs in newspapers and magazines, of awards and prizes and film sales.

When I talk to people like this, I try to suggest that it is very difficult to become a famous and fortunate Writer. Usually they will agree, because this is part of their dream. They believe that writing great fiction, or what is now called "creative nonfiction," will often be painful and wearisome. At first they may be lonely and misunderstood; but eventually, inevitably, they will be recognized and praised. They will have admirers and fans who will understand how hard they have worked and how much they have suffered, and will want to sleep with them, even they if are not very attractive or very agreeable.

Luckily, I have also met many people who do not say that

they want to be a writer. Instead they say that they love telling stories, or that they really like to write about practically anything. They like sending emails to friends describing the crazy weddings they saw on a trip to Niagara Falls, or reporting for their local paper about a brawl at a concert or political meeting, or an eccentric neighbor who makes sculptures out of antique farm equipment. They are curious about the world, even nosy, and have already found out that if you tell somebody—even a perfect stranger—that you want to write about them, they are usually happy to talk.

Most of these people will go on writing because they enjoy it. Most will be published, too, one way or another, since the world is full of print and Internet, newspapers and magazines that need material. They will publish articles and reviews and essays about nature or sport or books or films or their own and other people's lives, whatever is needed at the time, or interests them. Some of them will become professional journalists, and some will also write stories and novels and plays. A few may even become famous; but if they don't, they won't really care, because for them, most of the time, writing is fun.

All the pieces in this book were fun for me to write, too.

PERSONAL HISTORY

Nobody Asked You to Write a Novel

All young children are imaginative and creative; and while they remain young, these qualities are usually fostered. Their grubby but delightful paintings and verses and stories are extravagantly admired, shown to visitors, tacked to the kitchen walls. But as children grow older, encouragement of imaginative creation is often quietly replaced by encouragement of what have begun to seem more important traits: good manners, good marks, good looks; athletic and social success; and a willingness to earn money mowing lawns and baby-sitting—traits that are believed to predict adult success.

Children who seem unlikely to do very well along these lines sometimes find that their work stays on the kitchen wall longer than usual; and so it was with me. I was encouraged to be creative past the usual age because I didn't have much else going for me. I was a skinny, plain, odd-looking little girl, deaf in one badly damaged ear from a birth injury, and with a resulting atrophy of the facial muscles that pulled my mouth sideways whenever I opened it to speak, and turned my smile into a sort of sneer. I was clever, or as one of my teachers put it, "too clever for her own good," but not especially charming or affectionate or helpful. I couldn't seem to learn to ride a bike or sing in tune, and I was always the last person chosen for any team.

By the time I was eight or nine, I was aware of these disadvantages. I realized that I would never grow up to be an actress, a dancer, a model, an airplane stewardess, or even a receptionist. Luckily, none of these careers appealed to me. But it was also my belief that nobody would wish to marry me and I would never have any of the children whose names and sexes I had chosen at an earlier and more ignorant age. I would be an ugly old maid, the card in the pack that everyone wanted to get rid of.

I knew all about Old Maids from the Victorian and Edwardian children's books that were my favorite reading. Old Maids wore spectacles and old-fashioned clothes and lived in cottages with gardens, where they entertained children and other Old Maids to tea. They were always odd in some way: absent-minded or timid or rude or fussy. Sometimes they taught school, but most of their time was devoted to making wonderful walnut cake and blackberry jam and dandelion wine, to telling tales and painting pictures, to embroidery and knitting and crocheting, and to growing prize vegetables and roses. Occasionally they shared their cottage with another Old Maid, but mostly they lived alone, often with a cat. Sometimes the cat was their familiar, and they were really witches. You could tell which ones were witches, according to one of my children's books, because there was always something physically wrong with them: for instance, they had six fingers on one hand, or their feet were on backwards.

All right, that would be my future. I knew it was so because of the kind of positive reinforcement I was getting from adults. Just as with the Old Maids, all that I produced was praised: my school compositions, my drawings, my walnut brownies, my doll clothes and rag rugs, and especially my stories. "Charming!" "Really beautiful." "Perfectly lovely, dear." Nobody ever told me that I was perfectly lovely, though, as they did other little girls. Very well, then: perfection of the work.

Not that it seemed to me like work. Making up stories, for instance, was what I did for fun. With a pencil and paper I could revise the world. I could move mountains; I could fly over Westchester at night in a winged clothes-basket; I could call up a brown-and-white-spotted milk-giving dragon to eat the neighbor who had told me and my sister not to walk through her field and bother her cows. And a little later, when I tried nonfiction, I found that without actually lying I could describe events and persons in such a way that my readers would think of them as I chose. "Dear Parents—We have a new English teacher. He has a lovely wild curly brown beard and he gets really excited about poetry and ideas." Or, if he had written an unfavorable comment on my latest paper: "He is a small man with yellow teeth and a lot of opinions." Or any of two, three, twenty other versions of him, all of them the truth—if I said so, the whole truth. That was what you could do with just a piece of paper and a pencil; writing was a kind of witch's spell.

In my late teens, however, two things happened to disturb

my contract with the world. First, adults stopped saying how wonderful my work was, and I had to admit that they were right. I had by then read enough classic European and American literature to realize that by comparison my stories and poems were not really worth so much attention. Clumsy apprentice spells, they seemed, when set beside those of the great magicians—even when, as happened occasionally over the next few years, they managed to appear in print.

The other thing that occurred about the same time was that a few young men began to show an interest in me in spite of my looks. Maybe I wouldn't have to be an Old Maid after all, or at least not just yet.

I didn't stop writing; I had got into the habit of it, as someone else might get into the habit of singing in the shower. But once I was out of college, with a full-time job, writing gradually began to seem more like smoking or biting one's nails or listening to soap operas: a bad habit, a waste of time. It was something my friends and lovers thought I really oughtn't to do too much of, especially since I got so upset when rejection letters came, as seemed to happen more and more often.

Twice in my life I deliberately tried to break the habit of writing. The first time I was twenty-six; I hadn't had anything accepted for five years, and my first novel had been turned down by six publishers. Whenever I thought of this, which was several times a day, I felt as if I had an incurable toothache; and every day the toothache got worse.

On the other hand, I had not only found someone who wanted to marry me, I now had a two-month-old baby. My graduate-student husband, seeing how depressed and distracted I was, suggested that I should cut my losses. "After all, Alison, nobody asked you to write a novel," was the way he put it that late-spring day after breakfast, as he shoved a stack of corrected freshman themes into his briefcase, closed it, and set out for Harvard Square.

These words continued to echo inside my head while I did the dishes, and while I changed the baby, and tucked him into his carriage, and pushed him down towards the Charles River so that he could, as the phrase went then, "get some fresh air." It was a hazy warm May day. The lilacs were out along the fence, bundles of dark purple peppercorns opening into pale mauve stars. "Nobody asked you to write a novel," I repeated to myself. "You don't have to make up stories. You're part of the real world: you have a real baby and a real husband and a real house. Look how pretty the world is, and all you have to do is live in it."

I parked the carriage beside a bench and sat down on the grassy, sloping riverbank. The sun shimmered on the flowing water, and a white fishnet of cloud slid up behind the trees on the other shore. The words "fishnet" and "slid" crossed my mind, but I didn't try to stop them or scribble them down on the back of an envelope as I would have before, when I was a writer. There was no point in saving ingredients for new spells; I wouldn't need them anymore. Two people strolled by along the path: an oddly assorted couple, one very tall, taking long strides; the other much shorter and hop-skipping to keep up. I didn't speculate about them; I deliberately inhibited myself from imagining who they were or what their relationship was. "You needn't bother; you are free of all that now," I told myself. "You are normal, you are happy." I sat there by the water waiting to experience my new condition, to feel my freedom and normality and happiness, to be filled with it, to flow naturally as the river flowed and enter fully into Being.

But instead another sensation, very much stronger, came over me. It was a sensation of intense boredom. Now that I wasn't a writer, the world looked flat and vacant, emptied of possibility and meaning; the spring day had become a kind of glossy, banal calendar photograph: View of the Charles River. "This is stupid," I said aloud. I stood up and pushed the baby home and changed him and nursed him and put him down for a nap and went back to the typewriter.

The second time I stopped writing was more serious. It was two years later; I now had two unpublished novels and a batch of stories in a rejected condition. I also had two children in diapers and no household help. I had to write in the evening, when I was always tired and often miserable—miserable twice over because of guilt, for this was in the Fifties, when having a respectable husband and children was supposed to make a woman perfectly contented unless she was very immature, selfish, and/or neurotic.

This time it wasn't just my husband who suggested that I cut my losses, but also many of my friends and relatives did as well. Poor Alison, the consensus was, nearly thirty, hasn't had anything published in seven years. Obviously she's not a very good writer; she's never going to make it. Why does she wear herself out and agonize so? Why isn't she satisfied with her life? Today these well-wishers—most of whom did sincerely wish me well—would probably recommend that I take up some other, more practical, career interest. Since it was the era of Togetherness, they suggested that I ought to give more time and attention to my family.

Whenever I sat down at my desk, now I instantly fell into a depression. What had gone wrong with my writing? What made editors say that it "didn't quite come off," "wasn't really for us," "didn't sustain our interest," and all the rest of the mealymouthed, damning phrases? Evidently, what we had been taught was true: a woman had to choose between a family and a career; she couldn't have both, like a man. By marrying, I had lost my powers. I had published two children, but my two novels had been born dead.

So I gave up being a writer. I really did it this time: not experimentally for an hour, but deliberately and for over a year. Instead of writing I threw myself into Togetherness the way I might have thrown a bone to a nasty dog I had to make friends with. I organized family picnics and parties and trips; I made animal cookies and tunafish casseroles; I took my children to the supermarket and to the playground; I played monotonously simple board games with them and read monotonously simple books aloud; I entertained my husband's superiors and flirted with his colleagues and gossiped with their wives.

I told myself that my life was rich and full. Everybody else seemed to think so. Only I knew that, right at the center, it was false and empty. I wasn't what I was pretending to be. I didn't like staying home and taking care of little children; I was restless, impatient, ambitious. Somehow, because I was clever, or because they were stupid, I had fooled people into forgetting my appearance. I passed in public as a normal woman, wife, and mother; but really I was still peculiar, skewed, maybe even wicked or crazy.

For thirteen months this was my private state of mind. Then a friend in Boston, V. R. Lang, died suddenly. Bunny Lang was one of the founders of the Poets' Theatre, a gifted poet, playwright, and actress whose eccentric vitality had made existence more interesting and more difficult for everyone she knew. It was my first such loss, unexpected and senseless: as if some giant child's hand hovering over a board game the size of Massachusetts had grabbed Bunny at random and thrown her away. The game went on as if she had never existed. Somehow, people managed without her; they began to forget her.

Disturbed, even frightened by this, I decided to put down everything I could remember about Bunny as fast as I could, to save it, before I too began to forget. I didn't expect that anyone else would care about what I remembered, much less that it would ever be published.

While I worked, not worrying for once about whether my sentences would please some editor, I experienced a series of flashes of light. First, I noticed that I felt better than I had in months or years. Next I realized that I wasn't writing only about Bunny, but also about the Poets' Theatre, about academia and the arts, about love and power. What I wrote wasn't the whole truth—I couldn't know that—but it was part of the truth, my truth. I could still cast spells, reshape events.

As I went on, I began to see that the point of Bunny's life was that she had done what she wanted to, not what was expected of her. She knew perfectly well that most people thought her difficult, immature, selfish, neurotic—yes, sometimes even wicked or crazy. But this was, for her, at most a recurring annoyance. As far as I could tell, it had never occurred to her to arrange her behavior so as to be approved of or suit the current idea of what a woman should be.

Also, and finally, I realized that I too was not immortal. Any day I could be snatched off the landscape; and if I were, I would disappear without having ever lived my own life. What I wanted to do was write. Very well then, that was what I would do, even if—as then seemed probable—I would never again be published.

In the end it did not turn out like that. I was lucky. Two years later, friends who had read my memoir of Bunny Lang paid to have three hundred copies of it privately printed. Two years after that the brother of another friend gave his copy to an editor at Macmillan, and this editor accepted my third novel, one written for my own pleasure, almost without hope of publication. Finally, after another thirteen years, the memoir itself appeared as the introduction to a collection of V. R. Lang's poems and plays.

Of course this is not the end of the story. Nor is it just my story. Not all writers are born with their feet on backwards, but most of them, in my experience, sometimes feel themselves to be witches or warlocks, somehow wicked, somehow peculiar, somehow damaged. At least until recently, this has been especially true of women, who in order to go on writing have had to struggle not only with the ordinary evil spirits of economic necessity, editorial indifference, and self-doubt, but also with the fear that they are not "normal"—however this word is currently defined. In the past it meant staying home and keeping house happily; today, more often, it means having an absorbing job. But in both cases the underlying demand is the same, just as it is for most men. It is a demand that is always fatal to a writer: work, conform, accept, succeed; forget your childish impulse to play with words, to reimagine the world.

Their Harvard

Not mine, certainly. For Radcliffe students in my time the salient fact about Harvard was that it so evidently was not ours. We were like poor relations living just outside the walls of some great estate: patronized by some of our grand relatives, tolerated by others, and snubbed or avoided by the rest.

Almost every detail of our lives proclaimed our second-class status. Like poor relations or peasants, who might carry some contagious disease, we were housed at a sanitary distance of over a mile from the main campus, in comfortable but less grand quarters than those of our male contemporaries. Just to get to the Harvard campus meant a long walk—and during the icy Cambridge winters a very chilling one, since slacks were forbidden outside the dormitory. These were also the days before fleece-lined boots and tights: instead we wore buckled or zippered rubber galoshes over our saddle shoes, and wool knee socks or heavy, baggy cotton stockings that left many inches of frozen thigh exposed under one's skirt.

Though we took the same courses from the same professors, officially we were not attending Harvard, and we would not receive a Harvard degree. For the first year or two we would be taught in segregated classes in a Radcliffe building. Later we might be allowed into Harvard lectures, but once there we were invisible to many of our instructors, who continued to address the class as "Gentlemen" and would not see our raised hands during the question period. Possibly as a result, few female hands—or voices—were ever raised in a Harvard course. Most of us supported the status quo by keeping our hands in our laps. When a female classmate attempted to attract the lecturer's attention, we raised our eyebrows or shook our heads; we considered such behavior rather pushy, possibly a sign of emotional imbalance.

For, like most poor relations, we knew our place and accepted it with only occasional murmurs of dissatisfaction. It didn't strike us as strange that there were no women on the Harvard faculty or that all our textbooks were written and edited by men. We didn't protest because we could not use the Harvard libraries, join the Dramatic Club, or work on the *Crimson*; rather, we were grateful for organizations like Choral and the Folk Dance Society that were, for practical reasons, coed. In midnight heart-to-heart sessions we decided (and I recorded in my journal) that though girls were "just as important to the world" as men, they were somehow "not really equal." But semantics says it all: we were "girls" and would be girls at forty, while every weedy Harvard freshman was an honorary "man."

Despite these disadvantages my friends and I were not unhappy in Cambridge. Most of the time we were in a mild state of euphoria. For one thing, even as poor relations our lives were luxurious by modern undergraduate standards, as well as in some ways extremely old-fashioned. (In case of fire, for instance, we were supposed to escape by climbing out of our windows and shinnying down ropes. We practiced this maneuver in the gym, and each room had a hook under the windowsill and a length of hemp coiled like a stiff, prickly yellow snake in the corner; but I doubt that all of us could have managed it in a crisis.) We had private rooms, cleaned and tidied by tolerant Irish maids; a laundry called for our dirty clothes every week and returned them carefully washed and ironed; we ate off china in our own dining room and sat in drawing rooms that resembled those of a good women's club.

We also felt lucky because, being female, we were not fighting in Europe or the South Pacific. World War II was a central fact of adult life—it began on my thirteenth birthday, and when it ended, I wrote in my journal: "Its not being war is hard to imagine. There's a kind of childish haziness around it, so that being grown-up means there being war." Gas, meat, butter, and sugar were rationed; I delivered my ration book to the house mother on arrival each term. Finding a favorite candy bar or a box of Kleenex in a store was an achievement. We vied for the wafer-thin pats of butter refused by girls who were dieting, and often had to make do with tasteless white margarine that could not legally be tinted yellow. Our obligatory skirts and the rest of our clothes were made of scratchy recycled wool, skimpily cut in styles designed to save material.

Men were superior partly because they were, would be, or—later on and most impressively of all—had been in the war. Most of the boys we had gone out with during high school had joined the armed services, and those we met as freshmen usually vanished at the official draft age of eighteen and a half. As a result, many of us sat home on weekends rereading and answering V-mail. Harvard Square and Harvard Yard were full of V-12 Navy officers in training, whom I observed as "marching in the rain with frog-like noises," and of ROTC students whose chant was mocked by us as "Hotsy Totsy, I'm a ROTC." One of the Radcliffe dorms had been taken over by the Waves, whose tight, unflattering uniforms and evident discomfort as they drilled on our snowy quad evoked both pity and awe.

As it is easy now to forget, we did not know which side was going to win the war. We all knew or knew of someone who had been killed in action, and there was always the probability that this list would get longer. If the Allies should be defeated, Cambridge and especially Radcliffe might be, as I wrote at sixteen, "doomed—considering the Nazi attitude towards educating women." I put it melodramatically not only because I was an adolescent but because the possibility was so awful to contemplate: already in my first term I believed Cambridge to be—I still think quite reasonably—one of the most agreeable places in the world.

Cambridge in 1945 was not the crowded, clamorous, glossy-chic shopping center it has since become, but a leisurely college town. When I read Gerard Manley Hopkins's lines on Oxford—"Towery city, and branchy between towers"—I had only to look out the window to see them illustrated. Commercial development of the Square had been largely halted by the war; the "base and brickish skirt" that surrounded Harvard as well as Hopkins's Oxford was still—like our own skirts—of very limited dimensions, and there were no concrete fortresses among the university buildings. The architectural elegance and natural charm of Cambridge were tremendous: the Yard in its dissolving fall gold or pale spring green (this was long before the invasion of Dutch elm disease); the lilac-overhung brick sidewalks and gray eighteenth-century or Victorian Gothic houses on Brattle and Garden streets; the clouds floating over the Charles River and the grassy meadows beyond. For anyone who had grown up in or near the average American city of that period, it was amazing to discover that a town, as well as the countryside, could be beautiful.

Equally amazing was the discovery that a town might be based not on the manufacture and marketing of shoes, ships, sealing-wax, or securities, but on the dissemination of ideas. We saw that it was possible to center one's life around knowing rather than around doing—to concentrate on understanding the world rather than on exploiting it. "Knowledge really is power in Cambridge," I wrote in my journal—naively, but not entirely so.

As it turned out, this axiom applied to us poor relations in a very practical sense. One of the most important things I learned in my freshman year was that there is a way over or under every wall. Many of my friends and I had come to Radcliffe intending to major in English. Now we discovered that if we chose instead to enter the then recently created field of History and Literature, we could get through the wall. We could take Harvard courses; we could range the stacks of Widener Library in a daze of excitement that I still remember; and we would have a Harvard professor instead of a Radcliffe graduate student for a tutor. As a result, many previously rather vague and arty young women suddenly developed an interest in history—an interest that, though initially feigned, often became real later.

To have a Harvard tutor, as it turned out, was not always

an advantage. Some professors were impatient with their young female tutees: my first, David Owen, dismissed my anxious and naive questions with the remark, "The trouble with you is you're a worrier, like my wife." He rapidly passed me on to Richard Schlatter, who (though I did not guess this) was far more worried than I, since he had just lost his job at Harvard and had not yet found another. Mr. Schlatter (we regarded it as vulgar to call our teachers "Professor"—or, worse still, "Doctor") gave me weekly assignments on the most radical documents of English history, but withheld his own opinions of these and all other writings. "I shall never get to know him, he never has answered frankly or openly to any question of mine," I wrote; had I been more perceptive at eighteen, I might have been less cross.

But in Joseph Summers, who became my tutor for the remainder of my time at Radcliffe, I was unusually fortunate, and knew it at once. We came from completely different worlds—he was a Southerner, a pacifist and a serious Christian—and I was his first *tutee*. But his knowledge of and enthusiasm for literature were so great, and his sympathy so real, that though then only twenty-seven he was already a magnificent teacher. To me and my friend Doris Wilk, he was known not as "Mr. Summers" but as "Tutor"—in other words, the real thing.

History and Literature majors at Harvard in the 1940s also got to hear some of the most famous professors of the time. This was the age of the bravura lecture, and we went to our classes as if to a combination of theatrical performance, sermon, and political oration—to be entertained and inspired as well as informed. Our professors were larger-than-life, even heroic figures, who provided not only interpretations of books and events, but dramatic examples of different world-views and intellectual styles. From among them we and our Harvard contemporaries formed our own views and styles. Clumsily but eagerly we adopted the opinions and imitated the manners of our favorite lecturers: the tense, passionate, personal commitment of F. O. Matthiessen; the scholarly brilliance and elegant flair of Harry Levin; the intense boyish seriousness of Henry Aiken. Some of us tried to combine two or more admired styles, for example the lively, gentlemanly romanticism of Theodore Spencer and the weary, gentle-manly sophistication of Kenneth Murdock. And these were only a few of our possible models; there were many more available, in many more departments—not to mention the large supply of eccentric and dramatic personalities among our contemporaries at Radcliffe and Harvard.

Not all our courses were theatrical events. At times we sought out odd and recondite subjects, partly out of an inter-est in them, partly because it meant that the classes would be small. One term, for instance, my best friend and I stud-ied the folk tale ("Fairy Tales 101" to us) with the celebrated Celtic leprechaun Kenneth Jackson, and cartography with the celebrated Hungarian gnome Erwin Raisz. As a result, I still know how to protect myself from witches and how to tell which way a river is flowing from an aerial photograph, should either necessity arise.

Being unable to see into the future, I had not only no desire for a career in cartography but no expectation of ever teaching either folklore or English (here I was wrong). Like most of my classmates, I did not want to go on to graduate school (if we had, most of us would have been disappointed, since quotas for women were tiny or nonexistent). When I arrived in Cambridge I was already determined to be a writer—without, of course, having any idea of the difficulty of the task. Harvard compelled me to read the best poetry and prose of the past, in comparison with which my own efforts suddenly looked very shallow and shabby; only the optimism of extreme youth prevented despair. As for the writing of the present, it was not covered in Harvard courses: in our anthology of English literature the fiction of "The Contemporary Period" ended in 1922 with Aldous Huxley. Harry Levin's course on Proust, Joyce, and Mann, introduced while I was at Radcliffe, was regarded by many as daringly, even dangerously, modern. Though fashions have changed, I think we were lucky not to have the writers of our own time predigested for undergraduates. We could feel that they belonged to us rather than to academia.

Even less attention was paid at Harvard to teaching the writing of fiction. At first the only course open to Radcliffe students was English A-1, given in a lecture room in Longfellow Hall. Our all-female class sat in rows facing the teacher, Robert Hillyer, a ruddy, plumply handsome minor poet whose manner seemed to us courtly but curiously vague; we did not suspect that he had a drinking problem. For several weeks he collected our papers, but never returned any of them. Instead he spent the hour reading aloud to us from books he admired, very slowly but with much feeling. Finally one day he entered the room, pulled from his briefcase what looked like all the work he had ever received from us, heaped it onto the desk, and sat down. We waited expectantly. "Yes—young ladies," Mr. Hillyer said, more slowly than ever. "Yer—all—such—nice—young—ladies. Only you can't write, y'know. Wasting—yer—time." Then he put his head down among our papers and passed out.

In my final year, however, Albert Guerard, who had just come to teach at Harvard, began to give what was to be one of the best fiction seminars in the country, and I was lucky enough to be in it. Among the other students were future novelists Alice Adams, Stephen Becker, Robert Crichton, and John Hawkes; I am sure that Guerard's advice and encouragement had a lot to do with the fact that so many of us in that small seminar ended up as professional writers.

Though History and Literature got us past the academic wall between Radcliffe and Harvard, other means were needed to scale—or illegally tunnel beneath—the social one. Radcliffe "girls" in the 1940s were separated from Harvard "men" both by custom and by law. Even as girls our status was low: the fashionable dogma was that we were all what would now be called "dogs"—ugly, charmless grinds. This view was constantly expressed in cartoons and humorous articles in the *Crimson* and the *Lampoon*, and was the source of many jests even on the part of those whose relationship with us was cordial. B. J. Whiting, the Chaucerian scholar, was so popular with the students in my house that we invited him to be the guest of honor at dinner. As he was seated, he looked at his plate, which was painted with a Chinoiserie design of grotesque exotic birds. "Ah," he remarked. "At Harvard we have pictures of the buildings on our china. Here, I see, you have portraits of your alumnae." Instead of resenting this, we all laughed appreciatively.

A Harvard man who took out one of us poor relations was apt to be scorned or pitied by his peers. Quite evidently he lacked the personal and financial resources, or the spirit of adventure necessary to seek farther afield. He had been unable to procure a more glamorous date from Wellesley, Smith, or some fashionable junior college; he didn't even know some hometown honey willing to travel to Cambridge to see him. This official attitude had more effect on our morale than it did on our lifestyle. Propinquity has its advantages, and most of the Radcliffe undergraduates I knew dated Harvard students; of those who married, three out of four married Harvard men—a statistic that was known to us and often quoted.

As an institution Radcliffe made certain rather halfhearted attempts to maintain these figures. Every term each house held what was called, in an odd use of British slang, a "jolly-up"—it would now be described as a record hop or mixer. These occasions, for which invitations were issued rather indiscriminately, were nonalcoholic—though once in a while some guest would manage to spike the weak purple-pink punch. They tended to be unproductive of jollity, and girls who were already "going with" someone or had any pretensions to sophistication tended to avoid them—not always successfully, for our housemother and our social chairman pressed us to "be good sports" and "support the house" by attending.

We were also encouraged to have weekend dates by the nature of Friday and Saturday night dinners. At these meals wartime rationing was much in evidence, and we were served dishes described ambiguously as Vegetable Timbales, Shrimp Wiggle, or Carrot Surprise—this last a very nasty surprise indeed. We were thus strongly motivated to go out, but only for a limited time. Freshmen had to be in by ten every night; sophomores and juniors could stay out until twelve on weekends, and seniors till twelve any night. In order to leave the house after dinner it was necessary to sign out in a large public ledger, noting one's intended destination and time of return. At ten o'clock the doors were locked, and any "men" who might be visiting had to leave. Needless to say, men were allowed to visit only in the public rooms on the ground floor. Upstairs, the approach of any male—a plumber or electrician, for instance—was announced with warning shrieks: "Look out! Man coming!" It is not surprising that an unofficial anonymous poll taken while I was at Radcliffe disclosed that two-thirds of us were virgins.

Harvard, more tolerant or perhaps only more cynical, allowed women in its undergraduates' rooms, but only before six in the evening, and only providing that the door remained slightly ajar. The latter requirement was not always met; and even when it was, few Harvard proctors were ungentlemanly enough to shove a nearly closed door further open and peer within. The result of this system, predictably, was a generation of Harvard and Radcliffe graduates accustomed to making love in the afternoons—a habit that was to cause considerable inconvenience to some in later years. We often wondered about these rules; didn't the Dean of Students know that sex could take place before supper? It only occurs to me now that they may have been intended to limit mating behavior on class principles, since they discouraged Harvard students from carrying on relationships with the young women who were secretaries at the university or worked in shops around Harvard Square.

The Harvard and Radcliffe parietal rules, like the academic ones, were permeable to a combination of information and determination. Excuses could be invented, proctors could be eluded; confederates could sign a friend in at midnight and open the door to her later. In Eliot Hall, for instance, there was a student room on the first floor that had a window opening onto the back terrace. The window was covered by a heavy metal grating, but it could be unlocked from the inside in case of fire—or to allow ingress and egress after hours. Occasionally it was opened to admit a midnight guest. This room was much in demand by adventurous and independent young women; one of its occupants during my time later worked for a brief period as a high-priced call girl, while another became an English duchess.

In one way or another, many of us got over or under the wall that separated Radcliffe from Harvard in the 1940s, when Cambridge was still a college town. The wall, however, did not fall down—indeed, it seemed as if it would stand forever—and none of us thought of Harvard as ours. Today the Square is a vortex of high-rise construction and commercialism. The wall has crumbled: male and female undergraduates share dormitories and dining halls, take the same freshman seminars, wear nearly identical clothes, earn the same degrees, and go on to graduate school together. Radcliffe students are no longer poor relations, but members of the family. When I tell someone in his or her twenties where I went to college, the usual response is, "Radcliffe? Oh, you mean Harvard." No, I want to protest, and sometimes do, I don't mean Harvard, but a quite different and separate institution, and one that—whatever you call it—no longer exists. For as it turned out, the Radcliffe I knew was in fact "doomed," just as I had feared in my freshman year during the war—not by fascist invaders, but by the forces of time and change.

WORDS AND WORLDS

What Happened in Hamlet

In 1974 Jonathan Miller invited me to watch rehearsals of *Hamlet*, the third in a season of "Family Romances" he was directing in repertory at the Greenwich Theatre. I said yes at once. I had been in love with England and English literature ever since I was a child reading E. Nesbit and Winnie-the-Pooh. When I first arrived, at twenty-three, it was like stepping into an alternative reality, a wonderful looking-glass world where people actually drove on the left and had afternoon tea. But I was a tourist, there only for a few weeks, as invisible to the inhabitants as they were unknowable to me.

Twenty years later I returned—this time, fortunately, with introductions from my editor and from friends who had lived in England. After six months as the wife of a Cornell professor on sabbatical, I was more enchanted than ever. I returned as often as I could, renting apartments for a month or more almost every year. I began to meet people who had just been names in the book sections of newspapers and magazines. (Not bold-face names, back then: almost none of them were as well known as they later became.) Among them were Jonathan Miller and his wife, Rachel. Jonathan had made a splash in the review *Beyond the Fringe* and was now starting to be known as an innovative director. I was keen to discover what he would make of what is probably the most famous play in the English language, and how he would express his thoughts, using not words but a stage, lights, scenery, and actors.

I was also interested in how a stage production is put together, and in what professional actors are like—who they are, where they come from, and how they learn to pretend to be alternately kings and tramps, heroes and saints, lovers, madmen, fools, and murderers. Would these people and their world be different from the amateur actors and little-theater groups I had known in America, or the same? (The answer was: essentially the same, only more so.)

I began going to rehearsals, starting with the first meeting of the company in Greenwich in February 1974, following them to a hotel off Earl's Court Road for rehearsals a week later, and finally back to the theater. I talked to the cast and had lunch with them; I sat in the audience at the first preview, and drifted around backstage on opening night.

JONATHAN MILLER

He is usually compared by journalists to a large untidy sea bird, a stork, or, more accurately, a heron; mention is made of his height, his long legs and wings, prominent beak, and rumpled feathers. Photographs reproduce this accurately; what they cannot show is that he operates at a different film speed from other people; that he thinks, speaks, and moves noticeably faster. Often he is mentally or literally two impatient steps ahead of everyone else. As a director, this gives him great advantages. He can, for instance, see everything that is happening in a scene involving eight characters.

But speed and intelligence are not enough. Directing is an exhausting job, requiring a great deal of energy and willpower. In rehearsal there are essentially no times when Jonathan is not on stage, nothing and no one he can afford not to attend to. Sometimes he stands back like a painter from his canvas, but more often he watches from nearby in the crouched position of a runner, balancing on his toes, then sprinting forward to stop the action. He explains rather than demonstrates, not imitating the intonation or gesture he wants, but describing it. This is deliberate. "I don't want anyone to parrot me," he told me on the first day. "I want them to find their own way."

A successful director is, almost by definition, someone with a strong ego. There are times when, in order that his ideas shall prevail, Jonathan will use every weapon at his disposal: wit, charm, threats, praise, flattery, bribery, patience, impatience, argument, and scorching ridicule. There are times when all those weapons fail, and he goes home at the end of the day not only exhausted but, for the moment, beaten.

Wouldn't it be easier, I ask, for him to play a part himself?

"No. I could never be an actor, because of my stutter. I was all right in *Beyond the Fringe* because there I could improvise. The stutter only comes on when I have to give a prepared speech, or say lines someone else has written."

"A protest against anyone's telling you what to do?"

"Yes, perhaps." He looks away, is silent.

THE FIRST DAY

In the theater at Greenwich. It has the haunted, dingy look of all empty public rooms, and is also quite dark and very cold—economy and the fuel crisis having combined to extinguish all heating except during performances. Everyone is huddled in winter coats in the front rows while Jonathan, hunched on a box at the edge of the bare stage, delivers what he has called "a general brief chat" and turns out to be an elegant two-hour monologue full of erudite references and in-jokes.

"I want to make this production clear and diagrammatic." he begins. "Get away from all the romantic clutter, all the romantic fog." The set (by Patrick Robinson) will be absolutely simple—plain benches at the corners and center of the half–arena stage, and fixed screens at the back made of ropes strung vertically. The costumes (designed by Patrick's wife, Rosemary Vercoe) will be sixteenth-century, but subdued—blacks and browns with slashes of color, based on the portraits of Titian. (Jonathan leans forward to show and then pass round a book of reproductions.)

In line with this conception, Jonathan goes on, he will not try to make the Ghost look like a supernatural apparition. "Death isn't a disease which makes you misty, hollow-voiced, and ten feet tall. A ghost is simply, and horribly, somebody who shouldn't be there; somebody who has broken his contract and then suddenly comes back on stage during a performance."

Claudius, he continues, should not be played as a lecherous monster, but as a Renaissance prince who, like so many others, has murdered his way to the throne—and consolidated his power by marrying the queen. He is not in love with Gertrude, or she with him; instead she is terrified and fascinated—but not sexually, rather as a bird by a snake. (This interpretation is to cause much trouble later: it contradicts not only theatrical tradition and Shakespeare's text, but Irene Worth's and Robert Stephens's stage personae. During rehearsals there will be a continual attrition of Jonathan's version of the King and Queen, so that by opening night there is, to say the least, a strong undercurrent of sexual feeling between them.)

Basically, Jonathan announces, this is a play about the conflict between thought and action, "the standard Renaissance dilemma." On the one hand you have Hamlet and his university classmates Horatio, Rosencrantz, and Guildenstern—young men trained in the scholarly and courtly virtues. (Here follows a lightning exposition of the traditions of the Renaissance gentleman, with references to Castiglione and Sir Walter Raleigh.)

On the other hand you have Claudius and Gertrude and their court, concerned with worldly power and authority. Here problems are practical rather than theoretical, and the important human relationships are those of husband and wife, parents and children, rather than scholarly and Platonic friendship between men. "I don't mean they're buggering each other," Jonathan adds hastily. "It's an intellectual thing. . . . A conflict of generations. For Hamlet and his friends the world of the court represents corruption. It's something they have to reject, or come to terms with or, like Rosencrantz and Guildenstern, maybe be seduced by power and become killers."

PETER EYRE

"I'm very excited about the idea of doing *Hamlet* with Peter," Jonathan said to me before the production began. "He's one of the most conscious and intelligent actors I've ever worked with, and also one of the most sensitive and intuitive. Any good actor can project a strong emotion. Peter can do that, and he can also convey two conflicting emotions at once, a situation which is much more common in real life, especially in this country.

"But beyond all that he has a quality that's very very, rare in the theater. When you see Peter, you don't say, What a wonderful actor. You don't get the feeling he's acting at all, but that he's just an ordinary person who's got on to the stage somehow. At first the other actors are always thrown off by him. He hasn't had the same training, so he's always stumbling into them, breaking up their patterns, because he doesn't know the rules. That can be corrected in rehearsal, of course. But this time I don't want to correct it entirely, because that's the role of Hamlet in the play."

"I don't have to explain Hamlet's speeches to Peter," Jonathan tells me later during rehearsals. "What I have to do is to get him to speak the verse properly, musically, without losing that quality he has of seeming to think aloud." This will mean a lot of work, he says, but it is absolutely essential. "And besides, it will be good for Peter to work hard."

In Jonathan's view, Peter is now at a point in his career when he may become—and he actually did become—one of the best actors in England. The trouble is that he has too much money and knows too many fashionable and purely decorative (or in cruder terms, rich and idle) people, who encourage him to waste time and remain only a brilliant amateur.

Others besides Jonathan have plans for Peter. He will become their friend, their lover, their child; they want him to read their favorite books and see their favorite films. Robert Stephens (Claudius), who goes to a gym twice a week to work out, will invite Peter to come with him ("All he needs now is to get into condition, build some muscle"), Irene Worth (Gertrude) wants to cook him dinner and give him a bath. He gets fan letters from strangers in remote London suburbs who feel that he is their soulmate and beg or demand a meeting.

Yes but, what is Peter really like? Wishing to avoid the sort of projection I have just described, I will only say that he is a tall, thin, pale man in his early thirties, who looks about ten years younger than he is. He is much subject to illness, real and imaginary. (During the first week of rehearsals, he and everyone else was in a state of anxiety because he was spitting blood, but X-rays proved negative.) He is one of the eight children of an American businessman and an English aristocrat; he was born in New York, educated in England, went to drama school in Paris, and has already appeared with the Old Vic and in plays and films.

Peter has wanted to do *Hamlet* since he was a child, when his governess taught him and his brother and sister to recite scenes from the play to their parents. "I think now that playing Hamlet will be like being analyzed for the fourth time," he told me when we were having lunch in his tall thin house full of contemporary art in Kensington, before rehearsals began. The fourth time? "Yes. I've had an Adlerian analyst, and a Freudian, and a Jungian—he was by far the best." After the play has opened, I ask him if it has in fact been like an analysis. "Oh. yes. It made me think about my parents, and my father's death; about brothers and sisters—about suicide, especially. . . . But isn't that what it's supposed to make everybody think about?"

BACKSTAGE

For someone who has spent most of her time in theaters sitting out front, it was amazing to see, that first day at Greenwich, how shabby and makeshift things are backstage. Just out of sight of the audience are mops, brooms, and coils of rope; you descend the back stairs into an area of dingy cement corridors, naked lightbulbs, rickety folding chairs, wire coat hangers, and spilt powder. The common loo provided for the women in the cast is like what you might find in a railway café: small, cold, and dark, with a damp gray-veined sliver of soap on the edge of a bare washbasin—far inferior to the loo for ladies in the audience.

When the company moves into London, conditions are even worse. There, for four weeks, rehearsals take place in the White House Hotel in Earl's Court, in a large draughty square ballroom, once grandly Victorian. Now the cut-glass chandeliers and gold-framed mirrors are broken and dusty, the whipped-cream scrolls of plasterwork chipped and stained, the pink brocade loveseats as grubby and hamstrung as old Victorian whores. On fine mornings a weak sunlight leaks into the room through tall dirt-streaked windows—and also a steady, damp, penetrating cold which the single tiny electric heater cannot touch. "It is a nipping and an eager air," as Horatio keeps saying: the temperature in the room, like that outdoors, varies between six and ten degrees centigrade.

The actors rehearse in coats and scarves, and there is a tendency for them to stand with arms folded for warmth even in scenes where other gestures might be more appropriate.

But nobody complains. It is not English to mention physical discomfort, and besides there is an economic crisis.

It occurs to me finally to ask whether these working conditions are approved of by the actors' union. But apparently this is not the sort of thing British Actors' Equity is concerned with. They have other matters on their mind, as the Equity Deputy, or shop steward, for this production explains to me. And they are not in a very good bargaining position vis-à-vis management—of the Equity members in the country, over half are out of work at any one time.

It seems right that this Deputy should turn out to be Lionel Guyett, the serious, handsome young actor who appears at the beginning of the play as Marcellus, and again at its end as Fortinbras—both soldiers, examples of orderly authority. Lionel volunteered for his job on the first day of rehearsals, and he has been Deputy for several other productions. His duties are to keep an eye on the management to make sure that they do not break any rules, as by asking the cast to work more than ten hours in a single day, and to collect Equity dues. He has had a quiet time with this play, but things are not always so easy, what with actors who never have any ready money and managements who try to avoid paying overtime.

THE DUEL

An expert has been brought in to choreograph the fight in the last act. He is Bill Hobbs—a slight, spare, flat-faced man with the instant reaction time and sinewy stripped-down build of a

tennis pro, who travels all over Europe staging duels and battles. He has a thick folder of scripts for fights, with stage directions and diagrams ("Laertes—cut to head. . . . Hamlet—parry
with rapier. . . .") which he goes over with Jonathan.

Bill's job is complex, for the weapons and movements must
be historically correct as well as looking realistic. It is also quite
dangerous. Theatrical swords and daggers are blunt-edged,
but they must appear sharp and heavy; an awkward thrust can
cut your hand badly, or even blind you. Bill has already been
injured several times by clumsy dramatic swordsmanship, he
tells me. "It is probably just a question of time," he says, shrug-
ging and grinning, "until some ass gets me again."

The appearance of Bill Hobbs in the dusty rehearsal room
has a marked effect on the men in the company. Even those
who will not draw or carry a sword in *Hamlet* get up and
move around, play with the practice foils, and make jokes
about their own or each other's clumsiness. Uneasy anecdotes are recalled—that time in Chichester when Smith cut
up Jones's face so badly he had to leave the cast, while Smith
took over his (much larger) role. Standing armed opposite
each other for the first time, Peter and Nicky Henson, who
plays Laertes, exchange a nervous glance. But Bill knows his
job. By the end of the second week, the fight scene is so good
that when the rest of the company sees it for the first time,
they break into applause.

ROBERT STEPHENS

What I notice first is his physical presence, the impression he
gives of being more alive than other people—as if his body,
like Jonathan's mind, ran at a higher metabolic rate. As he

moves about the room, I have the sense that this is an exceptionally large, strong, handsome, healthy human animal, the kind that wins ribbons at county fetes.

Along with this good health goes unusual good nature, a ready interest in and affection for the rest of the company. "I like having Robert in a show," Jonathan tells me, "not just because he's a fine actor, but because he's so good for the general morale." Even when he isn't on stage himself, he watches the rehearsal closely, and is generous with praise and suggestions afterwards. As he talks to the others, he stands close to them, often with his arm round their shoulders; he hugs or kisses them as they arrive or leave. ("It's like being kissed by a cross between sandpaper and a sea anemone," Jonathan remarks.)

If Robert's own morale is good, it may be because of his sense of his own good luck. He began acting as a child in the back streets of Bristol, where his father was a laborer: putting on plays with his friends and charging the neighbors a halfpenny admission. When he told his mother that he wanted to be an actor, she was horrified. Actors, to her mind, were no better than gypsies and tramps. "'Why don't you go on the tugboats like my uncle?' she said to me. 'That's a good, steady, honest job.' But I didn't listen to her." Robert laughs—as if still, after years of success, he is surprised by his good fortune, like a man who wakes up every morning to discover that he has won on the pools.

At intervals during the production Jonathan worries about Robert: about whether his high spirits are growing too high to be safe or healthy. He also worries because Robert is what is called "a slow study." It takes him a relatively long time to learn his lines, and still longer to get fully into a part. At first he is puzzled by the role of Claudius, and keeps asking questions.

"Why do I say that?. . . How do I feel about Polonius?" Jonathan's psychological explanations make him frown, but his face lights up when Jonathan says "You want a businessrnan voice here, very fluent, comfortable, full of knowing authority. You're telling him. 'Well, just between us—as a matter of fact I have four of my chaps on the planning board.'" "I love Jonathan," Robert told me later. "I'd go through flood and fire for him."

THE GENERAL ELECTION

Following the British election of February 1974 the Labor Party, under Harold Wilson, came to power, replacing the Conservatives and their leader, Edward Heath. Both before, during, and after polling day, conversation about this national event is at a minimum, reinforcing my sense that actors live in a separate dimension. What comments there are deal wholly with Heath's and Wilson's diction and acting style, not their policies. Thorpe is rated superior to both of them in performance, and it is suggested that he might do well as Uncle Vanya. A straw vote taken by me two days before the election predicts a small Labor victory, with the Liberals a close second and twenty percent of the company undecided or not telling—leaving out Irene Worth, who says she thinks most politicians disgusting and hasn't bothered to vote in years.

THEATRICAL ECONOMICS

Before I knew better, I assumed that most British actors were rich or at least comfortably off, living in regal grandeur or trendy luxury. This notion came from faulty association of ideas. When I saw them on stage or film, they were often wearing brand-new expensive clothes and living in large, bright, elegantly furnished rooms. Sometimes they were dressed like kings and queens and lived in castles. Also, more obviously, the actors I saw most often and heard most about were the most successful—the few who really did have three cars, a town house, and a farm in Provence.

But beyond these few are a great many who are not very comfortable. The British Equity Association minimum rate of pay for a West End production is less than most secretaries earn. For the Greenwich productions, classified as "Subsidized Repertory," the Equity minimum is less than the pay of a bus conductor. And these rates are for public performances; rehearsal pay is still lower. Jonathan is popular with his company because he insists on full performance pay from the first day of rehearsal, but this is unusual.

Most of the company of *Hamlet* earn more than the Equity minimum, but not very much more. A few earn several times as much; but this sounds better than it is, since almost no actor in England works continuously. It is quite usual to be unemployed for half the year, and many members of the cast were out of work for months before this production started. And it must be remembered that these are not typical Equity members, but exceptionally talented and successful ones.

How do they manage to live at all, then? Mainly by selling themselves to films, television, radio, and advertising, where the pay scale is higher. Nicola Pagett (Ophelia) comes in late to rehearsal one day because she has been excused to do a "voice over" for a TV commercial. Eventually, while romantically colored views of Italy are flashed on the screen, she will be heard reading aloud a thirty-word script which she now repeats in a burlesque bedroom voice for us in the hotel bar: "The moon . . . the pines . . . my first Campari!" For this morning's work Nicola will receive more just in "expenses" than she earns in a week at Greenwich, and every time the ad goes out on TV, she will get another £3.

The easiest way to make a lot of money is by appearing in a well-known TV serial. The danger is that if it gets to be too well known, no director will cast you in a play. Philip Lowrie, the gentle, thoughtful actor who plays Horatio, was in *Coronation Street* from 1961 to 1968, then quit and spent the next four years without work. "They kept inviting me to come back on the show," he tells me. "I played Dennis Tanner, he was this sort of lovable layabout, but I'd got to absolutely hate him, and I knew if I didn't stick it out, I was done for."

Other members of the company make ends meet by posing for magazine advertisements or reading lectures on educational TV. Nicky Henson (Laertes) has appeared in gangster and horror films with titles like *Psychomania* and *Vampira*. "It was so bloody bad," he tells me of another such film, "that I was terrified it would become a camp success. But thank God, so far nobody's heard of it."

In effect, Jonathan tells me, Nicky and the rest of them are literally subsidizing the British classical theater by taking jobs like these—buying themselves time to appear in plays like *Hamlet*, *Ghosts*, and *The Seagull*. Jonathan Miller is doing the same thing. He is paid a flat fee of £600 to direct these three plays, or about £50 per week—often a fifty- to sixty-hour week, since Equity doesn't protect directors from overwork. He buys this time by directing films for TV and contracting to write popular books and articles. Usually he is behind on these contracts; on opening night, for instance, I found him in the stage manager's room simultaneously trying to listen to the play as it came out of the loudspeaker overhead and to type an overdue chapter of his current book.

IRENE WORTH

More than anyone else in the company, she looks and behaves like the popular notion of an actor. A leading lady in the grand tradition: I can imagine her photographed soft-focus, swan-breasted in classical draperies on an Edwardian sepia postcard. When rehearsal stops, the others turn off that invisible energy charge that makes them seem larger on stage than they are in real life. Irene does not turn it off. She is always on stage, as if she had no other personality: she orders cottage pie in the hotel bar with the resonant diction and eloquent gestures of someone who thinks five hundred people are watching.

And according to report she has no other private self or private life. She lives, in the old-fashioned phrase, completely for her art. Unlike less single-minded actresses, she has not managed (or cared) to accumulate jewels, country houses, husbands, children, relatives, or hangers-on. As far as anyone can tell me, she appeared fully formed on stage in the premiere of Eliot's *The Cocktail Party*, as Celia, the beautiful young religious martyr—taking on at that moment, perhaps, something of Celia's character, if not her destiny.

Like Celia, Irene Worth believes utterly in the importance of her mission. Nothing else matters. Called upon to die of poison in the last scene of *Hamlet*, she crumples onto the cold, filthy, bare floor time after time, without any evident thought of what is happening to her pink angora sweater. Other actors find her difficult to work with at times because of this single-minded intensity, and because of her freely expressed scorn of anything she considers artistically shoddy or conventional.

Considering Irene's reputation, and her undoubted brilliance as an actress (which everyone in the company admits, even when they are furious at her), she does not appear on stage very often. This isn't just because some directors are afraid of her temperament. Irene also turns down all roles and plays that do not meet her standards. She is interested in experimental drama, in improvisation. "I want to be where the theater is new, alive—at the moving edge," she says, with a gesture which indicates that this edge cuts like a knife. Then she tells me, her eyes shining, of the moment recently when she came nearest to Celia's famous martyrdom on the anthill: in 1971 when she toured the Near East in Peter Brook's production of *Orghast*, a play by Ted Hughes written entirely in an imaginary emotive language and presented before native audiences in a tent.

I was surprised to learn from *Who's Who* that this great lady of the British theater was born in rural Nebraska fifty-seven years ago. (It even seems strange that she should be of any definite age; she looks barely forty some days and nearly seventy on others, and has the gestures and walk of a young girl.) Yet in her passionate devotion to Art, Irene recalls other actresses and dancers who came out of the rural American Midwest, such as Isadora Duncan and Loie Fuller. When I try to imagine her childhood, I see Model T Fords and feed stores and dust blowing through empty small towns and out across an endless prairie. I think of Dorothy Gale in

The *Wizard of Oz*, and wonder what sort of cyclone it was that carried off Irene Worth.

ACTING AS A CASTE

What I have been told is true—the theater is a world apart, with its own language, history, and culture. It has its leaders and heroes (the name "Laurence Olivier," by my count, is invoked twice a day on the average). But socially at least, all actors are equal. Within the theater, the barriers of class—which to an American sometimes seem to turn the English social landscape into a tiresome maze of muddy quagmires and thick thorny hedges disguised with roses—hardly exist. There is no electrified fence between Robert Stephens, whose father was a builder's laborer, and Jonathan Cecil (Osric), the son of Lord David Cecil—one of whose ancestors, Lord Burghley, was Secretary of State to Elizabeth I and a probable model for Polonius.

To become an actor is often to step outside one's class into a separate caste. Two members of the company, however, have not had to do this, because they were born into theatrical families. Antony Brown (Polonius) is the son of a man who worked in vaudeville with Charlie Chaplin and Kate Carney; his grandfather was stage director at the Gaiety Theatre. He is an actor in the old comic tradition, and looks the part: he has the bald domed head and chin beard of figures in classical farce, and when he smiles, his mobile face becomes the classic comic mask.

Nicky Henson is the son of comedian Leslie Henson. After his father's death, he tells me, his relatives warned him against going into the theater; there were already too many starving actors, they said. So instead Nicky entered the stage management course at RADA. But he wasn't able to stay backstage; he began singing with a rock group, and then appeared in a musical. "The first night I opened in a real theater, my mother was there, and when the curtain rose she started weeping. . . . No, I wouldn't want my own kids to go on the stage, it's much too chancy economically. Of course, if they insist, what can you do?"

If there is a difference between Antony and Nicky and the rest of the cast, it is that they take being in the theater more easily. For them it is less of a sport and more of a craft; they know how to do it the way other men know how to lay bricks or remove an appendix. Both of them are married to actresses, and they are much involved in their families. When I met Nicky, he had just arrived at the theater on his motorcycle, and looked like the toughest guy in a gang—square-jawed, unshaven, in boots, jeans, studded jacket, etc. But the first thing he did after unstrapping his helmet was to pass round photographs of his two-year-old daughter and tell how, upon seeing her first snowfall that morning, she had remarked indignantly, "Dirty birds."

THE THEATER AS A TRADITION

Not only class barriers, but age barriers, are dissolved within the theater. Between the youngest and oldest members of the Greenwich company there are more than fifty years: Graham Seed is twenty-three; while both Anthony Nicholls and George Howe are well over the age at which people in most jobs are forced into retirement, yet they are still valuable to a director.

Their presence in the company is also valuable to the

other actors, especially in the early awkward days of rehearsals. It seems to promise that this clutter of anxious people in a
cold room will eventually turn into a production of Hamlet,
part of British theater history. Tony Nicholls, a tall, calm, dis-
tinguished-looking man, whom Jonathan describes to me as
"a real theatrical gentleman," has appeared in almost every
play Shakespeare ever wrote. At the first reading, where the
rest of the cast are turning pages and stumbling over strange
words, Tony speaks the Ghost's lines in a clear, resonant voice
and without a book, for he has played the part often before.
It is literally as if a spirit from the past spoke, inspiring and
blessing the enterprise.

George Howe, who looks like a very wise, cheerful, and
attractive gnome, has an even longer history as a Shake-
spearean actor. He first appeared in *Hamlet* in 1934, and has
twice played Polonius with the Old Vic Company in a castle
at Elsinore. At lunch breaks he, like Tony, is surrounded by
younger actors listening to his (sometimes scandalous) anecdotes of the theater.

As for Graham Seed, this is his first speaking part in a
London production—or rather parts: he is not only Barnardo
and the Player Queen, but a priest in the graveyard scene. He
plays them all with a childish seriousness and constant delight
in simply being on a stage, which is also important to the rest
of the cast, and sometimes cheers them up on dark afternoons.
Graham is here because Jonathan noticed him at Chichester
in a production of *The Taming of the Shrew*. He was one of a
bunch of Petruchio's servants who had no lines, and nothing
much to do but move furniture. At rehearsals it was obvious
that all of them were bored and impatient, except for Graham.
While the others went through their duties mechanically, and

talked and smoked and read the papers between cues, Graham watched what was happening on stage. "I didn't say anything to him at the time," Jonathan tells me. "But I made a note of his name, and I remembered him later."

NICOLA PAGETT

Why has this good-looking, well-brought-up girl, out of so many like her, become an actress? She has natural gifts, of course: a good figure, a musical voice, and the right kind of looks. Seen up close she is tiny, with a bright, doll-like prettiness and eyes almost too large for her face: on stage or film she becomes an incandescent beauty. But to be where Nicola is at twenty-nine you need talent, ambition, and endurance; you have to prefer the uncertainty and hard work of the theater to the security, ease, and comfort you might have if you married one of the successful young men who buzz round beautiful rich girls.

Perhaps some of the cause is in her past. Nicola was born in Cairo and brought up in Egypt, Cyprus, Hong Kong, and Japan, as her father, a Shell Oil executive, was transferred from one office to another. From twelve on she spent part of every year at school in England, traveling half round the globe alone on airplanes. The idea that there are many different worlds in which you must play different roles was familiar to her very early. She didn't acquire a love of travel, though; she says now that she doesn't ever want to leave England again. "Of course if I had to go on tour, that'd be different. I'd feel safe anywhere in the world with an acting company round me."

Nicola is very happy with the Greenwich production. "It's every young actress's dream; three parts like these, with a director like Jonathan," she tells me. But early on in rehearsals her ideas about Ophelia conflict with Jonathan's. She wants to go round the stage in her mad scene kissing people and giving them flowers, while he insists upon a sterner and more complex interpretation. "Ophelia's a girl who doesn't know who she really is; who lets other people, men, define her. When they're knocked off one by one—her brother gone, her father murdered, Hamlet out of his mind, as she thinks—she cracks up, she retreats into childhood. Schizophrenic regression. I want her to ignore everyone else in the room, to suck her thumb and play with dolls, like my daughter Kate did at three." Nicola frowns and protests, but Jonathan wins in the end—and the reviews will bear him out.

Yet he knows how to do more than impose his will: he can bow to necessity and turn the limitations of an actor to advantages. He does this for Nicola when it turns out in a later rehearsal of the mad scene that she has great trouble learning or carrying a tune. As she falters again and again, the rest of the cast try to help her: at one point Irene, Robert, Philip, and Nicky are all singing at her simultaneously, in perfect pitch, but to no avail. Nicola panics. "How should I your true-love know, know, kno-ow, no, no!" she cries. "It's no use. I can't do it." Jonathan comes to the rescue. "Don't try to get it right. Go ahead and hesitate like you just did. let it go flat, that'll be marvelous."

ACTING SCHOOLS

A noisy discussion at lunch in the hotel bar on this subject. In general the younger actors speak well of their training, while the older ones call it a waste of time or worse compared to practical experience. Robert Stephens gives a scathing imitation of the mannerisms of candidates for the Old Vic, and George Howe thinks standards have fallen since he was at RADA in the early twenties and learned his trade from real professionals like Claude Raines instead of theorists who wouldn't last one night in weekly rep.

With much laughter, mimicry, and trading of mock insults, it is explained to me that RADA produces flashy sophistication ("You may not get the best instruction, but you get a good agent, and learn how to light a cigarette on stage in the West End"). LAMDA teaches earnestness of purpose and intense belief in The Theater and your own roles. Central is currently the most technical, with classes in singing, dance, mime, and stage accents.

Condemnation and ridicule of the Actors' Studio style of training is general. "I don't care how somebody feels about a part—that's between him and his conscience," Jonathan says. "What I want is an actor who can say a line eighteen different ways. I am not running a clinic." Yet a few minutes later he is talking about the relation between his current job and the one he was trained for. "Directing and diagnostic medicine are mirror images. In both cases you're concerned with small physical signs which connote deep inner states. But you work in opposite directions."

THEATER SUPERSTITIONS

These are famous, of course. Putting your shoes on a table or whistling in the dressing room are bad luck. Worst of all is using the word "Macbeth"; it must always be referred to as "the Scottish play'" and the leading actor must be called by his first name during rehearsal. Even if these rules are followed, the play is unlucky, and there is a long tradition of disasters occurring during production. Beyond these specific superstitions, there is a general readiness to believe in the supernatural, or at least the uncanny. During the nunnery scene, Peter is supposed to snatch from Nicola's hands the rosary she has been holding, and throw it to the floor. In rehearsal, one chilly dark day, he does this with such vehemence that it slides across the room into a far corner. At the next break Nicola goes to retrieve the rosary, but she cannot find it. A full-scale search develops; furniture and objects are moved, but the thing has vanished, perhaps down a crack in the skirting board. "It's a small miracle," Jonathan says. "The first of many." There is general uneasy laughter and jokes about God's displeasure with this production; finally Jonathan promises to get the rosary Nicola will use in the play deconsecrated.

THEATRICAL MAGIC

Dramatic theatrical experiences have a strange effect on many people. In the intermission at an Oscar Wilde play I and my friends seem to speak in epigrams, and on the way home from a suspense film the streets are full of sticky shadows and suspicious delivery vans. And this occurs after only an hour or two. The same thing can happen to those who must speak the lines we have only heard, day after day in rehearsal, and then night after night.

Already, just a few weeks into rehearsal, there are moments when the mood of *Hamlet* appears to dominate the company. Even the "sickness imagery" noted by the scholar Caroline

Spurgeon seems to affect them, so that presently not only Peter but also many of the other actors are or have been ill, and there is much talk of symptoms and remedies. The rehearsal hall also begins to look like one of the spare ballrooms of a rundown Scandinavian castle; the actors lounging round it like disaffected courtiers who most of the time have no occupation, but dare not leave for fear of the king's displeasure.

When I silently question something Jonathan has told them to do (as when he tells Peter to deliver a soliloquy lying flat on his back), he begins to look like Claudius—an upstart who has usurped the throne of the dead ruler (Shakespeare). At other moments, when I approve of his direction and feel that the actors are wrong to object to it, Jonathan looks like Hamlet, a noble mind driven half-mad by the ignorant stubbornness or self-seeking hypocrisy of the people about him.

On the cast, the effect of the play is even stronger. Infection of an actor by the personality he assumes is a traditional occupational hazard of the theater. It isn't supposed to happen in a repertory season, where Petruchio cancels out Macbeth and vice versa. But this season is different. In each of the three Family Romances, Irene Worth plays a dramatic and dominating woman with some secret in her past; Robert Stephens her lover, revealed in the course of the play as a phony if not a villain. Peter Eyre is her brilliant, sensitive, neurotic son; and Nicola Pagett, in each case, is an intense young girl, baffled in her love for Peter, who is superior to her in rank. And Antony Brown, as Nicola's father, provides homely wisdom and comic relief.

Of all this lot, only Robert Stephens seems to have escaped infection, and have nothing in common with Claudius, Manders, and Trigorin except his worldly success and sexual energy. Others, off stage, appear at times to merge into their roles. Irene's need to be stage center, Peter's illnesses and subtle wit, the jokes and theatrical anecdotes Antony tells at tense moments, come to seem quite natural—and I am not really surprised to observe that Nicola, as she kneels at prayer during the rehearsal of Act II Scene I, is simultaneously mending the lining of Peter's overcoat.

THE PLAY SCENE

In other productions it has always seemed to me slightly pointless and contrived. Now it begins to have many meanings. The Player King is not imitating only the bombastic actors of Shakespeare's time, but also, and quite deliberately, those of the recent British theater. "You've got to understand that there was a complete change after the last war," Jonathan explains to me. "The source of it was in the universities, especially Leavis at Cambridge. Before his students took over the British classic theater, it was all historical pomp and pageantry, trumpets and banners, with very little serious attention to the meaning of a play or its patterns of metaphor."

But beyond this, as Jonathan stages the play scene, it becomes clear that it is not just a theatrical in-joke, but a way of drawing us in. He has Claudius and the other members of the court turn their backs on us to watch the Player King and Queen, so that we become part of the real audience.

The implicit suggestion is that the audience at Greenwich will also be "struck . . . to the soul by the cunning of the scene" and recognize our own past misdeeds in it. What we are watching, of course, is a murder, but a very peculiar one.

The Player King, like Hamlet's father, is killed by having poison poured into his ear—as if Shakespeare were making a bitter and ambivalent joke about the power of words, his words—or our own—for good or ill.

OPENING NIGHT

Jonathan has tried to get round the usual anxiety by having a preview the day before, and putting the critics off until next week. It works only up to a point. By seven o'clock everyone backstage is highly keyed up. The dressing rooms are full of flowers and telegrams, and the actors, some in partial costume, are running back and forth between them. Irene, in the star dressing room below the stage, stays put, but Nicola, who is also solitary, finds it lonely, and keeps going into the large room shared by nine of the actors, where there is a lot of clowning and general high spirits.

Up the stairs at the back, where Robert, Peter, Jonathan, Cecil, and George Wood share a smaller room, things are more tense. Peter has been ill for twenty-four hours with food poisoning and is even paler than usual; as he crosses the room, he seems to tilt slightly sideways. He has twice as many flowers and telegrams as anyone else, but the telegrams are all unopened and the roses and irises and freesias still in their cellophane. ("I regard it as bad luck to read my telegrams until after the performance. Anyhow, tonight I can't spare the effort." He laughs rapidly.)

As the audience begins to file in, they can be heard in every dressing room over the sound system. The remarks of those nearest to the stage come through clearly above the general murmur (holders of front-row tickets please note). "Oh, darling, lovely to see you!" "Tell me, who is that strange man over there with Diana Melly?"

When the play begins, the actors stop talking among themselves and listen intently. They know where trouble is likely to occur, where a laugh may be expected. Halfway through the first court scene, when it is clear things are going fairly well, they relax, begin to speak of other things, read a newspaper, or play cards. But nothing holds their interest for long—they keep breaking off to listen to the resonant, emotional voices coming over the loudspeaker, which are interrupted at intervals by the calm, even, Scottish voice of Jeannie, the pretty girl who is assistant stage manager: "This is your call, Miss Pagett, Mr. Henson."

At intermission Jonathan comes into the dressing rooms to praise and hearten all the actors individually and report favorable comments he has heard in the bar. They seem encouraged, but not yet at ease. Nicola shuts herself in her room to practice feeling mad, and Graham Seed is frantically changing from one of his three costumes and makeups into another.

There is some relaxation, but not much, during the second act, and even more rushing about from room to room. Only at the end, when everyone in the cast is either on stage or waiting in the wings for their curtain call, is there finally silence in all the dressing rooms, broken only by a roar of long-awaited and long-continued applause.

THE FIRST-NIGHT PARTY

It is held at the house of Lady Antonia Fraser, the well-known London beauty and biographer (*Mary Queen of Scots*, *Cromwell*) who is an old friend of Peter's, and much admired in the company. There is a midnight supper of Edwardian lavishness prepared by Antonia's Scottish cook, Mrs. Hepburn—roast ham, turkey, duck, smoked salmon, etc. The actors, most of whom haven't eaten for twelve hours due to first-night nerves, crowd round the table hungrily. It is a motley gathering, which Antonia, in a long golden caftan, presides over like Titania at her feast. Besides the cast, there are rich and titled persons (what Jonathan calls "Peter's aristos"), journalists, drama students, star-crossed lovers, several elves and fairies, the Frasers' beautiful fifteen-year-old daughter Flora (barefoot in Pre-Raphaelite silks), and a genuine rag-and-bone man whom somebody found in a pub on their way to Campden Hill Square. I wander among them, feeling as if I had walked into a classic English novel of the sort I read long before, almost invisible but completely happy. The party goes on until dawn, long after I have left. The last guest is found asleep on a sofa at eleven the next morning, by the men from the caterers who have come to collect the rented champagne glasses and gilt chairs.

THE REVIEWS

These are mixed, as usual with Jonathan's productions, and cause the cast those sensations of delight, indigestion, and indignation one might have after a lengthy dinner combining rich spiced dishes with cold tinned slops. The play as a whole is described by the daily papers as "superlative," "eccentric," "bleak," "fascinating," and "enjoyable." Peter's performance is "exciting," "arbitrary," "neurotic," and "somberly intelligent." Similar contradictory adjectives are applied to most of the company. Robert and Irene are generally praised, but here, too, there is contradiction: one reviewer sees Claudius as "self-tortured and conscious-stricken" while another speaks of his "cold, matter-of-fact defensiveness."

It doesn't matter, really, because *Hamlet*, and indeed the whole Greenwich season, is already sold out. Still, everyone feels better on the weekend, when the *Sunday Times* comes out with a long brilliant rave review by Harold Hobson, who calls the production "extraordinary. . . . an absolute revelation of the meaning of a play that we wearily thought we knew backwards and forwards."

AFTERWORD

The play goes on at Greenwich, but Jonathan Miller's part in it is over, and he is not sorry. "It's been by far the most difficult production I've ever done," he tells me the next day. "And not only because Hamlet is such an important play."

One reason it has been difficult, perhaps, is that it is the sort of play that cannot help but reflect and stir up private feelings. Jonathan's original interpretation set the intellectual world of Hamlet and his friends against one of practical action and power represented by Claudius and Gertrude and the court, and it is not hard to find parallels. You begin with a group of university classmates, young single men writing or appearing in *Beyond the Fringe*. But as Jonathan says of Ophelia, "Not to grow up is madness." It is necessary to move on, to enter the real world—but this world is guilty, corrupt, and destructive. To act is to kill, since whatever you do will destroy the existing pattern.

I remember a day in Earl's Court when they were rehearsing the scene in which Hamlet and the Captain (in this production, Fortinbras) watch the Norwegian army pass. Jonathan got up and stood beside Peter and Lionel where the edge of the stage was marked on the floor with masking tape, and looked down as if into a deep valley. "You see them going by, twenty thousand men. The horses, the loaded carts, the guns on their carriages, the flags looped back over their standards. Twenty thousand men. Some are walking, some sitting on provision wagons—think of Mother Courage. You watch them passing, and you say to yourself, Why am I not acting, who have cause, when these men who have no cause are on their way to do something? Of course, the action they are going to do is murder."

However, there is a third way. You can engage the world indirectly, without guilt (or with less guilt) by interpreting it—by painting pictures or taking photographs—or, like me, writing articles in which, by a cleverly biased selection of details, you try to alter history so that people afterwards will remember a production of *Hamlet* as you have described it.

Or, more seriously, and with greater risk and reward, you can direct a play. At Greenwich, Jonathan gives orders and moves people around, but he does so in the service of an idea. "Directing is a mid-point between the world of the mind and the world of action. It's a narrow point—one is always balancing on a thin edge. But when it works right, for me, there's nothing like it.

The Language of
Deconstruction

Innovations in language are always interesting metaphorically. When the words used for familiar things change, or new words are introduced, they are usually not composed of nonsense syllables, but borrowed or adapted from stock. Assuming new roles, they drag their old meanings along behind them like shredded shadows. To the amateur observer this seems especially true of the language of the contemporary school of literary criticism that now prefers to describe itself simply and rather magisterially as *theory* but was at first popularly referred to as *poststructuralism* or *deconstruction*.

Many of the terms current in the field, like its ideas, originated in France, and their translation into English sometimes subtly altered their meaning. The earliest neologisms of the movement, Saussure's "significant" and "signifie," became *signifier* and *signified*, now employed to distinguish words (signifiers) from their meanings (the signified) and emphasize the arbitrariness of the terms we chose. The use of these particular terms (rather than, say, *word* and *thing*) underlined the seriousness of the process and its claim on our attention. Since in English to *signify* can also mean "to announce or portend," as in "the siren signified that a raid was coming," it was also possibly suggested that words predicted coming events—as indeed they did in this case.

With *deconstruction* we move into another and more complex realm of implication. The most common use of the terms *construction* and *deconstruction* in English is in the building trades, and their borrowing by literary theorists for a new type of criticism cannot help but have certain overtones. First, it suggests that the creation and interpretation of literature are not organic but mechanical processes; that the author of a piece of writing or "text" (see below) is not an inspired, intuitive artist or interpreter, but merely a workman who cobbles existing materials (words or signifiers) into more or less conventional structures.

The term *deconstruction* implies not only that the text has been put together like a building or a piece of machinery, but also that it is in need of being taken apart again, not so much in order to repair it as to demonstrate its underlying inadequacies, false assumptions, and inherent contradictions. This process can be repeated many times and by many literary hard hats; it is expected that each deconstruction will reveal additional flaws.

The preference for the term *deconstruction* rather than *criticism* is also interesting etymologically. *Criticism* and *critic* derive from the Greek *kritikos*, "skilled in judging, decisive." *Deconstruction* (Latin *constructus*, "piled or put together"), on the other hand, has no overtones of skill or wisdom; it merely suggests the demolition of an existing building. In popular usage criticism suggests censure but not change. If we criticize someone or something, we may condemn them but we do not carry out the sentence ourselves. The contemporary theorist, by implication, is both judge and executioner. When he or she is finished with a text, it will have been totally dismantled, if not reduced to a pile of rubble.

More recently, many literary theorists have made their position even clearer. Instead of the term *deconstruct* they use *interrogate*. Of course, when you "interrogate" anything, the implication is that it is under police custody. It is probably guilty of something (often racism, sexism, or fascism). It needs to be questioned and examined, perhaps with the kind of "enhanced interrogation techniques" now recognized as an euphemism for torture. Occasionally, a text may be *recuperated*, suggesting that it was perhaps not technically guilty, but merely ill, and that its crimes may be partially excused by a plea of temporary insanity.

Central to the new language of theory, and rich in association, is the word "text, which now appears even in the discourse of critics who fear and detest the new theories. The notion of using a single word to designate every sort of written message was innovative and practical; what gives a neutral observer pause is the term (or, if you prefer, *signifier*) chosen. In the past, critics spoke of stories, tales, novels, and poems: words that etymologically evoke a world of human lives and human creation. *Story* derives from the Greek and Latin *historia* ("narrative history"), tale from the Old English *talu* ("reckoning, speech") and the Old Norse *tala* ("talk, tale, number"). Novel comes from the Latin *novella narratio* ("new tale"), and poem from the Greek *poeima* ("something made").

Before deconstruction a *text* in common parlance was one of two things: a school textbook, or "a short passage from the Scriptures, especially one quoted. . . as the subject of an exposition or sermon." The expansion of the term to include all written works inevitably suggests to the uninitiated observer that literature is not intended to entertain but to instruct; a text is something we study under the direction of an authority. The discussion by Roland Barthes of "the pleasures of the text" may at first suggest an attempt to restore enjoyment (*jouissance*) to reading. But in practice this enjoyment seems to be both dependent on critical interpretation and directly related to a disregard of the author's intentions; it is a kind of guided erotic tour.

The word *text* derives from the Latin *texere* ("to weave") and *textus* ("a web; texture, structure"). The suggestion is of something made by a spider or a human weaver. Appropriately, the texts studied by theorists are approached not with any interest in their individual authors, but as examples of the mumblings of the *Zeitgeist*, as if they were the work of either an ignorant artisan or an anonymous arachnid. And indeed many critical papers give the impression that their authors are flies struggling in the sticky verbal strands of theoretical discourse.

If you are a theorist, for practical purposes, the author is irrelevant. The encounter is always with the sick, criminal text. Earlier schools of literary criticism have usually been interested in writers, sometimes even too intrusive—prying into their personal lives and their psychological and economic motivations. I have found it so. "Theory," by contrast, usually excludes them from consideration. In a way, this can be restful. The author of a guilty text is now no more to blame than those innocent girls in Salem who, when possessed by demons, screamed curses and blasphemies. When I was teaching at Cornell University, I once learned through the student grapevine that a new junior colleague would be using one of my novels in an undergraduate seminar on modern fiction. Assuming that this person was too shy to ask, I volunteered to visit the class and answer questions about my "text." "Oh, no thank you," I was told. "That won't be necessary." For pedagogical purposes, I did not exist.

Among teachers, even before theory, a "text" was usually expected to be difficult to access. Even today, when we study a physics textbook or the Bible, we are not supposed to be able to understand what we read without the help of a teacher or preacher. Literary theory expanded the definition of "text" enormously and critically. For one thing, redefining poems and novels and stories as texts removed them from occasions of private appreciation and set an interpreter between them and us. Many contemporary critics, like medieval churchmen, seem to prefer to stand between the text and the reader, blocking direct access and substituting their own commentaries or *metatexts* for their chosen Gospel. The tendency of some modern theorists to "read" the whole world as a text—a notion reminiscent of the medieval idea of the world as God's book—expands the area of the layman's presumed ignorance and the critic's wisdom and power.

Using the term *text* implies that a work is worthy of study, but it may also sideline it, since in both churches and classrooms a text has traditionally often been only the jumping-off point for a sermon or lecture which may range far afield. So it has been with the texts of deconstruction, which more often than not give rise to amazingly intricate and far-fetched *discourses*, another now popular word with both religious and educational overtones. At times it seems that the briefer the text, the more elaborate is the critical structure built upon it.

Many people have pointed out the practical advantages of the term *text*, which embraces every sort of written document from an advertising slogan to a verse epic. The hidden implication of this apparently generous and inclusive term, however, is that all texts are equal: the difference between the advertising slogan and the epic is one of social context rather than one of value or meaning. In practice, however, some texts are more equal than others: they are *privileged*. They deserve to be rewarded and honored and widely read. This term has also passed into common academic—and occasionally nonacademic—discourse. Outside the university, though, it is still most often associated with matters of social class, and for literary critics to adopt the term suggests that there is still rank among documents.

While texts are privileged, characters and concepts within them are more apt to be spoken of as *valorized*, that is, highly valued, but not always correctly. The term is almost always used in a negative, debunking way, to expose the hidden assumptions of a given text. But because most of us learned the word "valorize" ("to fix the value or price of a commodity") before we read literary theory, the old meaning haunts the new usage with its implication that what writers are doing in presenting any character or idea as admirable is equivalent to price-fixing. Echoes from the word "valor" also hint that there is something illegitimate in attributing "boldness or firmness; courage or bravery" to anyone or anything, since a reputation for these qualities must usually be won rather than assigned.

For theorists, it is not popularity or traditional acclaim (economic success or aristocratic lineage, so to speak) that now determines the value of a text; it is the decision of the literary critic. At first this might suggest that critics, like royal personages, assign the highest rank and title to selected members of the mob of texts suing for their favors. However, this is true only to a certain extent. Contemporary critics, like many sovereigns, tend to keep the greatest honors and privileges for themselves. Today it is critical theory that is truly "privileged." As Jonathan Culler put it in his lucid and thoughtful, if at times terrifying, survey of trends in the field, *Framing the Sign*, "formerly the history of criticism was part of the history of literature . . . now the history of literature is part of the history of criticism." The late Paul de Man even suggested that critical or philosophical or linguistic texts are fully as "literary" as poems and novels, which may account for the fact that many articles and books in the field seem, especially to a novelist or poet, intended not so much to supplement as to compete with the works they claim to discuss.

In some university courses today students read mainly critical theory, and class discussions revolve around such second-level texts. The fact that these texts, too, are subject to deconstruction, and their deconstructions to further deconstruction, has produced an exhausting series of commentaries on commentaries which recall nothing so much as the productions of medieval scholasticism. To the unconverted this mass of words resembles the infinitely retreating and dimming reflections in opposing mirrors.

More recent developments in poststructuralist criticism, and more recent verbal inventions, are too many and various for me to even attempt to cover. A thorough investigation, though, might look at the metaphoric suggestions of Derrida's *difference* and *difference*, and the daunting vocabulary of terms from classical rhetoric adopted by writers like Paul de Man and Harold Bloom, which suggest that literature is a form of political oratory, and that to write is essentially to pose or deceive.

Attention should also be paid to the emerging language of feminist criticism which, for example, sometimes speaks of women's writing as *fluant* ("flowing"), suggesting, unfortunately, that though spontaneous, it may also be damply emotional and unstable. Equally interesting is the vocabulary of the New Historicists, who lend to use the term *subversion* in the place of *deconstruction*, calling up a Conradian world of plots and counterplots, revolution and ruin. Several writers, both feminist and historicist, have been accused of *recuperating* (in this case, reviving) Marxist vocabularies and texts— thus by association implying that these terms and works were seriously ill, or perhaps even that literature itself is an illness.

To the common reader all these new vocabularies are daunting and confusing. Perhaps that is one of the aims of their inventors and users: many new intellectual disciplines, like elementary school cliques, tend to adopt their own private version of pig latin in order to build morale and confuse outsiders. Among these confused outsiders, unfortunately, is often the writer. Earlier schools of literary criticism have usually been either friendly and easily accessible, or if anything too invasive—prying into writers' personal lives and their psychological and economic motivations. "Theory," by contrast, excludes authors from consideration.

Before the present time it is unlikely that many authors of poetry or fiction or drama ever sat down to create a text.

Today, however, a few writers seem to be doing just that. They are deliberately producing work that is intended to be taken apart and studied rather than read and enjoyed. Some of their productions have been original and interesting, but most of them depress me and make me sorry for their authors, whom I see as trying in vain to run round the end of the new school of literary criticism and score some points for their own words. Even if what they say won't be taken seriously as a poem or story, or a statement of values, the hope is that it will qualify as a kind of criticism.

I am afraid that these writers are in for a disappointment. Critics have never taken kindly to attempts to usurp their functions; and though they may claim that their own work is literature, they are unlikely to concede that any collection of words put together by an author, including the present one, could be taken seriously as criticism.

My Name or Yours?

Feminism, like many other social movements, has had its troubles with language, and especially with names. We have learned to say *chairperson* and *humankind*, and are gradually managing to replace the ungainly pronoun "he/she" with the new multi-person "they" and "them," avoiding sentences like "Tell whoever has parked his/her van in my driveway that if he/she does not remove it I will report him/her to the police."

On the other hand, many women are still not sure what to call themselves. For centuries wives were concealed from the world behind their husbands' names. You were Miss Jane Smith until you married; you then immediately became Mrs. Thomas Brown. Few people who weren't personally acquainted with you knew your first name, or dared to use it if they did. The name "Mrs. Thomas Brown" was generic and transferable; it did not designate a particular individual, but merely "the current wife of Thomas Brown." At the time this seemed completely normal to us. In the 1960s I and a group of friends put out a cookbook to raise funds for the nursery school our children attended. All the recipes were signed with our married names: I was Mrs. Jonathan Bishop.

Today, most of us would probably sign our recipes with our first and last names. but we would expect to be called Ms. rather than Miss or Mrs. in our professional lives, partly because, like Mr., it does not reveal marital status. Miss or Mrs. is still used sometimes on formal private occasions: political banquets, society fund-raisers, and debutante balls. It is also favored by women whose only public identity is that of the wife of their (often well-known) husband.

Even today, it is common for women to take their husbands' last names, especially in conservative circles. Problems start later. If your husband dies, you will still be Mrs. Thomas Brown, a respectable widow. But if you are divorced you automatically become Mrs. Jane Brown, thus informing the world that your marriage has failed. Tommy Brown, of course, never has to change his name, and can conceal his marital status all his life. If he remarries, another woman will immediately become Mrs. Thomas Brown.

If you were especially daring, or especially angry at Tommy, you could petition to resume your so-called "maiden" name. There were difficulties with that choice, however. Many of my divorced friends kept their husband's last name so that it would continue to be the same as that of their children, or because it was associated with their public or professional identity. Some, too, had been glad to lose their original name. It is no fun for a little girl to be called Susie Hogg or Susie Mudd, and an acquaintance once told me that one of things about her first husband she liked most was that his last name was not Fink.

In the nineteenth century many women writers were known by their husband's name only; some of the best-selling novels of the time were announced on their title pages as "By Mrs. Clfford" or "By Mrs. Oliphant." Later, the usual thing to do when you published your first book was to use your first name and your husband's last, as if you were already divorced. Of course, if you actually got divorced later, you might find yourself stuck with the last name of a person you disliked or even hated. Writers who did not marry, or started publishing early, like Willa Cather or Mary McCarthy, were luckier. I was lucky too: though I had been married for fourteen years when my first novel appeared, I decided to stick with my original name because I knew it would please my parents. I had no wish to please my mother-in-law, and anyhow there were already far too many writers called Bishop.

In the second wave of feminism in the 1960s and '70s, young women were encouraged to reject their patronymics—"slave names" was the term used by the most radical—and choose new surnames. Sometimes these honored the maternal line: Polly the daughter of Joan might become the photographer Polly Joan; she might have decided instead to be Polly Joans, Polly Joanchild, or (in a feminist version of the Icelandic custom) Polly Joansdaughter. Other women adopted the name of the state or city in which they were born or lived, like the artist Judy Chicago. Another popular choice was the month or day of one's birth: Jane March, Susan Monday. You could also choose a name linked to your occupation or hobby: Mary Weaver, Ellen Fern.

All this was fine. Problems came later, when these feminists married. Many, even those who had been content to bear their fathers' names, balked at the idea of dissolving their identity in their husband's. A temporary solution, at the time, was to hyphenate the surnames of bride and groom. The pairings were not always ideal, as in the case of friends whom I will call Ann Fish and Bill Gold. For one thing, there was the question of whose name would come first. They could of course alternate, so that individuals called Ann Fish-Gold and Bill Gold-Fish would come into existence. This was sure to cause confusion in doctor's offices and at work, let alone when Ann and Bill tried to rent an apartment, buy insurance, or set up a joint bank account. Usually, therefore, the choice was to put the husband's name first.

There was potential trouble, too, when the children of hyphenated couples grew up and fell in love. Ann and Bill Gold-Fish were very happy when their daughter Jenny fell in love with Jerry, the intelligent and attractive son of friends whom I will call the Good-Littles. They were not surprised when the kids refused to become Jenny and Jerry Good-Little-Gold-Fish. Obviously, they would want to shorten their name, but which of their four parents would they symbolically reject? As it happened, Jenny and Jerry decided to solve the problem by discarding all four last names and adopting a brand new one, Tompkins, after the county in which they lived. This not only slightly hurt and embarrassed both sets of parents, it also involved tedious public announcements and legal proceedings.

Worse things have happened. A romantic couple I knew of, when they married, chose the last name of Joy. It was not prophetic, and two years later they split up. As a result, both of them had to go through lengthy, expensive, and somewhat mortifying procedures to restore their former names to their bank accounts, credit cards, drivers' licenses, web addresses, and much, much more.

Today many brides have returned to the practices of a much earlier generation and become what my mother would have called "Lucy Stoners," after the nineteenth-century feminist who refused to take her husband's name. When they marry, they keep their surnames. But again, what about the children?

Fortunately, there is a simple solution to this problem, which I should like to recommend to everyone. In anthropological terms, it involves setting up a system of parallel matrilineal and patrilineal lines. Under this plan, both husband and wife will pass their own surnames on to all children of the same sex: boys will take their father's last name, and girls will take their mother's. If this sensible and equable custom is adopted, both women and men will have names that are theirs for life. It will be a sign to the world that marriage is an equal contract in which no one's identity has to disappear. Eventually, this plan will also greatly simplify record-keeping and the work of genealogists. Daughters will be valued as much as sons, since they will also preserve a family name, and also, in some European countries, a family title.

Indeed, the idea seems so simple and intelligent that, if humans were rational beings, I would look forward to seeing it adopted throughout the world. My enthusiasm, by the way, is wholly philosophic and disinterested. As the mother of three sons, I would still be doomed to see my surname vanish under the enlightened new system as surely as it will under the antiquated patriarchal customs of the present.

Witches Old and New

Over the years I have met many people who considered themselves to be witches and/or worshippers of a female deity, whom they usually referred to as The Goddess. They were of every age and social class, and of both sexes—though, as in the witch trials of the sixteenth and seventeenth centuries, women predominated. With one exception, all claimed that they were good, or white, witches, and worked only for positive ends. They celebrated the seasons of the year and the power and glory of nature. They cast spells to find lost objects; to bring health, wealth, love, happiness, and peace of mind to themselves and their friends; and occasionally to block the evil or misguided actions of institutions such as the Internal Revenue Service, the Pentagon, and Cornell University.

The one witch I've known who admitted to a less benign use of her magic arts was the writer Shirley Jackson, best remembered now for her brilliant and frightening short story "The Lottery." She did not always claim to be a witch, but she also did not deny it, sometimes giving examples. At one time, she told me, she and her husband, the critic Stanley Edgar Hyman, were extremely annoyed by his publisher, Alfred Knopf. "Unfortunately, my powers do not extend to New York State," she informed his secretary and several other acquaintances. "But let him be warned. If he enters my territory, Vermont, evil will befall him."

The warning was passed on; but several weeks later, rashly disregarding it, Knopf took a train to Vermont to go skiing. The first day he was out on the slopes, Jackson said, he fell and broke his leg. After emergency medical treatment, he was helped onto another train and returned to his territory, Manhattan.

Had Shirley Jackson lived four hundred years ago, she might well have been accused of witchcraft as a result of this incident. It follows what the Oxford historian Robin Briggs proposes as a common pattern. A feels him/herself to have been injured, cheated, or slighted by B—or perhaps merely gives B a peculiar look, or makes an ambiguous gesture. Soon afterward B falls ill, has an accident, or suffers some other unexpected misfortune. B, and B's friends and relatives, blame A, who is probably a witch.

Briggs's scholarly and agreeably written book includes many such cases. Unlike some historians, however, he is also deeply interested in "the belief system that made witchcraft credible" and persecution possible. What he has set out to do, he writes, is "as much to reconstruct a way of thinking and living as to offer explanations for the great persecutions of the sixteenth and seventeenth centuries." At times the perceived effects of witchcraft seem to be as delusional as the accusations: one woman, Jacotte Simon, for example, "believed she was bewitched, because several rat-sized animals seemed to be running about inside her body." In another case, early one morning when Simon was still asleep, two "marvelously big and ugly" cats, whom she later identified as two of her neighbors, appeared at the end of her bed. "Although she could not move, she managed to make the sign of the cross with her tongue, calling out to her husband for help." When he rushed in, they vanished "with a great noise."

As Briggs and others have pointed out, our primary sources for these events are fragmentary, skewed, and unreliable, since they consist almost entirely of trial records and confessions obtained as a result of threats and torture. Nevertheless historians have come up with a variety of definitive, sometimes contradictory, explanations for the phenomena: economic, political, social, and religious.

Robin Briggs's approach is far more modest. He politely remarks that few of the theories of other historians "are wholly worthless," though it is clear that he considers many of them extremely limited. Again and again he apologizes for his inability to come to definite conclusions, since the evidence is so patchy, compromised, and contradictory. Yet in spite of these continual disclaimers, his book on the subject, *Witches and Neighbors*, contains several interesting observations. Its title, for instance, is descriptive rather than exclusive. According to Briggs, most accused witches were neighbors and/or close acquaintances of their accusers. Also, as a rule, episodes of witchcraft persecution were not "essentially directed and managed from above" by the authorities, as some historians have claimed. Instead, they were the end result of long-term, small-scale social and economic conflict and superstitious belief. Today, Briggs remarks, "many people deal with social conflict as the African nomads did; they move on or find new groups to associate with." Meanwhile, in static communities all over the world, belief in witches flourishes.

Witches and Neighbors is based on an extensive investigation of sixteenth- and seventeenth-century data from Western, Northern, and Central Europe and New England, and also "a close study of nearly 400 trials from Lorraine" in eastern France. Anyone who has ever sat in a provincial library or courthouse, trying to read a very old document in a foreign language, written in crabbed handwriting and ink faded to burnt brown on crumbling paper, must feel awe and admiration for Professor Briggs and the use he has been able to make of this obscure and recalcitrant material.

The villages of late sixteenth-century Lorraine, as Briggs reveals them, seem to have been full to the brim of petty disputes and sudden ludicrous events:

> Claudon Colas Colin warned Jennon Etienne to keep her geese out of his meadow—She passed before his horses and held out her arms, whereupon one of them fell down, dying a few hours later.

Even representatives of the Church were not immune from these occurrences.

> The curé of Bisping had helped arrange a marriage and was roused early from his bed to join the party which fetched the bride. As they went on their way Senelle Fetter, whose own son had been an unsuccessful suitor for the girl's hand, was seen looking over her door at them. The curé started to feel unwell—He took to his bed with fever and a swollen leg, to die maintaining that she had given him the illness.

As Briggs points out, most societies studied by anthropologists or historians believe in witches. The only exceptions are a few nomadic African tribes, who developed witches as soon as they settled down. Witchcraft, his book suggests, is the outward manifestation of inescapable social conflict. If you live in the same place for several years, sooner or later one of your neighbors will do something that irritates you very much. This is even more likely if you are in direct economic competition with him or her, as early modern villagers were. If you, like almost everyone else in your village, believe in the power of spells and the evil eye, it is a short step to blaming your most unpleasant neighbors for whatever goes wrong.

If times are hard, Briggs remarks, fears and accusations of witchcraft seem to be even more common. This happened during the sixteenth century, when most people in Europe suffered a continuing drop in their living standards. Overpopulation reduced stocks of food and depressed wages; there was increased competition for scant resources such as wood for fuel: "Wages declined in real terms, work became harder to find, pauperization spread." Briggs compares the condition of the peasantry to that of "people trying to cling to a sharply inclined sandhill." Local misfortunes also played a part: "Devastating weather, plagues of insects, epidemics of animal disease and similar misfortunes might arouse villages or larger regions to peaks of anxiety."

When things went wrong in these communities, a common reaction was to look around for someone to blame. Usually the suspected witch already had a reputation for being difficult and easily offended, or unreasonably demanding. In a subsistence village economy it was taken for granted that you would help your neighbors out when things went badly for them, and that they would return the favor. Gossip and suspicion focused on people who openly envied and resented others' good fortune, and on those who frequently asked to borrow food or small sums of money but seldom returned the favor. Social slights were also apt to end in suspicions of witchcraft. The neighbor who was not invited to a wedding or a christening feast was frequently blamed for subsequent problems, especially if he or she showed resentment. As Briggs points out, this theme passed into folklore as the familiar motif of the excluded witch or fairy godmother taking her revenge.

Unusually persistent or ungrateful beggars were also very apt to be accused. In a world without organized public assistance, charity was a religious duty. Besides, the local beggars were often also longtime neighbors: people who in the past had been self-supporting, but were now too old, ill, or crippled to work, and had no relatives to support them. When times were hard, charity could become onerous. More and more often, the demands of aggressive beggars for money or food were met with refusal. And, as any big-city resident today can testify, beggars who are turned down often become unpleasant; they may even curse those who have refused to give. In sixteenth-century rural Europe, such reactions were taken seriously, and might be blamed for any subsequent misfortune, even if there had been no overt threat:

Margueritte Liegey, known as la Geline ("the hen"), had allegedly been a much feared beggar . . . for twenty years. After Claude George refused her alms one day she fell ill with her mouth twisted—

Most accused witches, according to Professor Briggs and many other modern historians, were very far from the skilled and powerful figures of folk belief, though in their confessions they—and their examiners—drew heavily on these beliefs. At first they usually denied being witches, or claimed that they only used their knowledge for good. It was only later, after long-drawn-out examinations which often included torture, that they confessed to having cast evil spells, signed a compact with the Devil, or attended witches' Sabbaths.

Public accusations of witchcraft, however, were in fact extremely rare. When people believed themselves bewitched, the most common reaction was to ask or force the suspected person to remove the spell by means of a gift, a touch, or a prayer. If he or she refused, or denied responsibility, one might try some do-it-yourself charms and prayers. The next line of defense was to consult an expert: either the local priest, or a "cunning man" or "cunning woman" who would confirm the identity of the culprit and cast a counterspell. (Cunning men and women, of course, had considerable prestige in local society, but since they were known to have special powers, they were also in danger of being accused as witches.)

As Robin Briggs points out, it usually took at least fifteen or twenty years of gossip and suspicion before there was a formal accusation, and the majority of cases never reached the courts. There were several reasons for this. First, whether or not you won your case, the accused witch and his or her friends and relatives were very likely to take revenge on you—either magically or materially. The accused person might also decide to declare that you, too, were a witch; you might then soon find yourself in the same prison.

Second, the economic consequences of a witchcraft trial could be devastating for the accuser. Traditionally the property of a condemned witch went to the state or local government to defray the costs of the trial, which might be very heavy. But if, as often happened, the witch was too poor to pay, the entire village (including the accuser) was liable for costs. If the witch was acquitted, the accuser might have to pay all costs, and could also be sued for slander. In some European jurisdictions, moreover, "it was still normal practice to imprison plaintiff as well as accused" until the initial depositions had been taken.

As a result, when there was a formal accusation it was common for several families or individuals to pool their grievances and suspicions, assuming probably that there was safety in numbers. Occasionally, Briggs relates, wholesale accusations were employed by the local political authorities to get rid of unwanted persons, usually vagrants and beggars—an early and drastic parallel to current denunciations of homeless and unemployed people, who (like witches) may be blamed for a wide variety of social ills.

Today, the popular stereotype of the witch is invariably a poor old woman. Historically, this is only partially correct. It is true that in the sixteenth and seventeenth centuries many witches were at the bottom of village society, or at least less well off than their accusers. Sometimes, however, the rich and powerful were accused—though usually by the even more rich and powerful, or their dependents. In such cases, the details tended to be extravagant. In 1588 the vice-governor of Trier was accused of having gone to the witches' Sabbath "in a golden wagon to urge the destruction of all the crops." "On other occasions he and his followers . . . brought on a terrible hailstorm that killed forty-six cows, by standing in a brook and pouring water over their heads in the name of a thousand devils."

The accused witches tended to be older than the average villager; but as Briggs points out, in most cases suspicion against them had been building for at least fifteen or twenty years, it must often have started when they were fairly young.

The idea that all witches were female is also an error. In many parts of Europe, Briggs says, "men comprised 20 or 25 percent of those charged; in some, including large areas of France, they actually formed a majority." (According to Briggs, in a study of modern rural France, where belief in witchcraft is still prevalent, one out of four suspected witches was male.)

Briggs's explanation for this gender imbalance is that women were and are apt to be poorer and more dependent, and that they were and are more apt to be associated with the family and the household: thus, domestic disasters such as the illness of a cow or a child are more likely to be blamed on them. He also points out that contrary to the belief of some contemporary feminists, midwives were less likely than the average woman to be accused, though they were often consulted when witchcraft was suspected.

Briggs takes pains to disprove other popular misconceptions about the persecutions of suspected witches. For example, he tells us that most estimates now put the number of people executed in Europe between 1450 and 1750 at forty to fifty thousand—not, as some modern writers claim, nine million. The persecutions were also far from general. Though most of the common people believed in the existence of witches, "a substantial majority of towns and villages did not experience a single trial, successful or otherwise, over the whole period."

Though many accused witches denied the charge, or confessed only under torture, Briggs thinks that some of them came to believe in their own powers. After all, if you already believe in witches, and the curses you utter in a moment of rage or resentment come true, maybe you're one of them. And if you have good reason to be angry, envious, or resentful—if you're poorer and less lucky than your neighbors—the idea that you have special powers can be attractive. As Briggs points out, though, the power of witches "was essentially negative, to drag others down with them." It is clear from the trial records that though the Devil might promise a witch wealth and prosperity, or the ability to heal others, he almost never came through on these promises. His only sure gift was the power to harm.

In England and Scotland, interestingly, the pact with the Devil was usually replaced by a compact with an animal familiar who was his representative. Frequently the animal was a cat, but dogs, chickens, ferrets, hares, toads, and hedge-hogs were also reported. Usually the witch was believed to suckle the familiar with her own blood—a striking instance of the traditional British devotion to pets.

Though most of Robin Briggs's tentative explanations of the witchcraft persecutions seem reasonable, he does occasionally propose psychological explanations that will strike some readers as limited. He suggests, for instance, that some people projected their own hostile wishes toward their relatives onto outsiders, and then called them witches. Parents, he says, sometimes feel but repress hostility toward their children; and children often wish that their younger siblings would die. If these people did in fact die, "fear and repressed guilt would then combine to direct suspicion at surrogate figures." This seems plausible, if impossible to prove; on the other hand, it is unlikely that most people would have felt repressed hostility toward a cow or a pig or a field of hay, and projected such wishes onto their neighbors.

Diane Purkiss avoids the problem of the confusing, fragmentary, and probably biased records of the witchcraft trials by putting aside any attempt to find out what "really happened" and concentrating on what people thought happened, both then and now. In *The Witch in History*, Ms. Purkiss, who is a Lecturer in English at Reading University, has interesting things to say about contemporary witchcraft, and some striking if idiosyncratic comments about earlier (mainly fifteenth- and sixteenth-century) material.

Some readers will be turned off:—and others, no doubt, turned on—by Purkiss's vocabulary. This is full of words like "problematics," "gender theory," "reify," "recuperation," and "valorize"—words that are like red petticoats to prestructuralists. When some people see these words, they become maddened and charge. I felt a little restive myself at first, and began to paw the ground, but gradually I calmed down.

In Part I of *The Witch in History*, Purkiss examines the beliefs of the contemporary witchcraft movement. Today most educated Americans and Europeans who identify themselves as witches or pagans, and many who are merely sympathetic to the movement, believe what Purkiss calls "a religious myth— The religion it defines is radical feminism." According to this myth, she says, in sixteenth- and seventeenth-century Europe millions of women who lived alone and worked as herbalists and midwives were accused of witchcraft and burned alive because their independence, sexual freedom, and medical knowledge threatened established religion and medicine. This myth, Purkiss points out, is also "often linked with another lapsarian myth, the myth of an originary matriarchy." Radical feminist historians, Purkiss says, treat the witchcraft myth as relevant not only to the past but to the present. They believe (with some justification) that male authority is still trying to suppress strong women— though evidently with more success in some parts of the world than others.

Though Diane Purkiss sees—and presents—the attractions of the witchcraft myth, she is also aware of its drawbacks. Her relation to contemporary witchcraft on the whole is ambiguous—as seems natural for a writer who confesses in her introduction that as a child her favorite book was *The Wizard of Oz*, and that she identified strongly with both Dorothy and the Wicked Witch of the West. At four, her favorite game involved pouring a bucket of imaginary water over her mother, who "gamely went through the motions of melting many times a day." (Robin Briggs, writing in a very different tradition, that of the very private British academic, only informs us by implication that he gets on well with his colleagues and likes his wife.)

Purkiss begins by describing the creation of the witchcraft myth in modern times. For example, she describes the transformation of the "action wing" of New York Radical Women, WITCH, from the potentially dangerous Women's International Terrorist Conspiracy from Hell of 1968 to "a mild-mannered bunch of consumer-rights groups" with names like Women Intent on Toppling Consumer Holidays and Women Inspired to Commit Her-story. As she says, "committing her-story is significantly less threatening than committing terrorist acts." The problem, in her view, is that far too often "herstory" becomes what she calls "hystery"—a false and melodramatic version of the past.

Purkiss also analyzes, rather critically, several modern literary versions of the witchcraft myth, such as those that occur in the poems of Sylvia Plath and Anne Sexton, where death by fire is embraced and sexualized—in spite of the fact that English and American witches were hanged and not burned. She appears to think better of Fay Weldon's rather frightening novel *Puffball*, in which the witch is wicked and spiteful, pointing out that this is the kind of story "early modern women themselves told about witches."

One distortion of the feminist witchcraft myth that Diane Purkiss particularly deplores is the attempt to compare the witchcraft persecutions with the Holocaust, in part by inflating the number of women who died. The most frequently cited figure in feminist literature, she says, is nine million. "Worryingly, this goes two million better than the Holocaust, as if a competition is afoot, and at times there does seem to be a race on to prove that women have suffered more than victims of racism and genocide (as though women have not been among the victims of racism and genocide)." Feminists like Mary Daly, Purkiss thinks, "seem unaware that the Holocaust itself bore more heavily upon women, who were much less likely to be selected for work and hence survival than young men, and who were gassed automatically if pregnant or nursing an infant." Such writers, Purkiss suggests, can sometimes become potential persecutors of women themselves, as when Mary Daly identifies nonliberated females as "fem-bots" (female robots).

The "myth of the Burning Times," Purkiss concludes, "is not politically helpful" because it portrays women as helpless victims, both in the past and in the present. This may be so in the long run, but it is also true that almost all political and religious myths, not excepting the one that is most popular in Europe and America today, include many stories of saints and martyrs who have died for a cause.

Diane Purkiss is also critical of the feminist myth of early European—and also contemporary—witches as midwives, herbalists, and healers, "gentle, maternal, close to the

earth." She rejects this myth first because it is too "close to
the conservative and even reactionary 'Heritage' culture of
thatched cottages, country churches, and spinsters on bicy-
cles." It is anti-urban and patriarchal, forcing women into
traditional, relatively powerless roles. (It also clearly excludes
the successful lawyer, doctor, or college lecturer who lives in
a high-rise flat and is too busy writing books like *The Witch
in History* to cook or garden. The end result is "to reify associations between women and the primitive, the uncivilized,
the instinctual." In some cases this may be true, but there are
many feminists who believe that women have always been
the more civilized sex—reading books and playing musical
instruments and embroidering tapestries while the men in
the family were away fighting stupid wars.

Diane Purkiss's analysis of the contemporary witchcraft
movement, like her analysis of their myths, though generally
critical, is occasionally and almost reluctantly admiring. She
points out that witchcraft is not a thing of the past, but exists
here and there in modern England and America in many
different forms. Purkiss does not attempt to classify these
forms, but Shelley Rabinovitch, in her contribution to James
R. Lewis's *Magical Religion and Modern Witchcraft*, has done
so most capably. Rabinovitch distinguishes three main types:
Religionist, Goddess Celebrants, and Ecopagans, though she
notes that many individual groups combine aspects of more
than one type.

American and British "religionist witches" usually describe
themselves as Wiccans: they are often "concerned with legiti-
mization of their belief systems as a bona fide religion." They
are the most hierarchical of the three groups, and the most
dependent on ritual objects and ceremonies, such as the burning of incense and the consecration of the elements of water

and salt; they focus on what Rabinovitch calls "power-over." Members of these groups tend to come from the ceremonial branches of Christian and other faiths. Religionist groups often include men, and the leaders of many are men—as in some I have visited in England and Ireland. Today, Wicca is recognized as a legitimate faith in parts of America; the State Prison in Auburn, New York, for instance, allows a Wiccan priestess equipped with a ceremonial broom to meet with inmates regularly for ceremonies.

God/dess Celebrants, Rabinovitch says, are extremely eclectic: they include Radical Faeries (all-male), radical feminists (all-female), and Dianic (coed, but mainly female) groups. They tend to be more loosely organized, lack formalized leadership, and favor poetic do-it-yourself rituals. Their main goal is "to free the participants, and through them society at large, from patriarchal restraints and assumptions." They focus on what Rabinovitch calls "power-from-within" and may also practice alone, like Shirley Jackson.

Ecopagans, though they may worship a god/goddess and celebrate the usual pagan holidays (the four solstices, May Day, Beltane, Halloween, etc.), are seriously concerned with social and environmental issues. Rabinovitch speaks of them as focusing on "power-with," and they often cooperate with organizations like Greenpeace, the Quakers, and animal rights activists. Tompkins County, New York, where I live, contains at least two such assemblies.

It is clear that for Diane Purkiss only Ecopagan witches are really admirable, and even they could improve. She praises the groups who took part in the antinuclear protests at Greenham Common, helped to halt road building projects through ancient forests, and challenged English laws against New Age travelers—laws which she sees as designed to keep "the undeserving poor" in the cities, leaving the countryside as a refuge for the upper and middle classes. But she also complains that "witches emerge only rarely from Pagan activities to make common cause with other women" in campaigns for equal pay or reproductive rights. In my experience this is not always so: often witches working on such issues deliberately conceal their identity so as not to compromise the campaign and cause bad publicity. At a rally for Planned Parenthood not long ago, I noticed several women in jeans and T-shirts whom I had last seen at a Winter Solstice rite in robes decorated with astrological symbols.

Some of Diane Purkiss's charges against modern witchcraft suggest a Marxist viewpoint. Witches, she says, do not recognize how deeply they are involved in "capitalism and consumerism." They buy unnecessarily expensive equipment for Wiccan rites, which is manufactured and sold through catalogs that list, among other items, "genuine black heavy cast-iron traditional three-legged cauldrons," when in fact one's own largest well-used cooking pot would probably be at least as powerful. Moreover, many of their magic spells are "actually narcissistic rites of self-contemplation." Rituals are valued as bringing psychic health; the emphasis is on changing oneself rather than altering the world, and "the self constructed is the familiar self of late capitalism."

In spite of her many criticisms, Diane Purkiss ends her survey of contemporary witchcraft and its myths with the suggestion that feminist historians might learn something from modern witches, and a self-critical and rather odd postmodern vision of what might be the consequences:

> A feminist history which sought to draw on the strengths of this movement rather than simply pointing to its weaknesses might be excit-

ing. . . . It might be speculative, unreliable, often wrong, sometimes ridiculous, politically very useful, . . . and absolutely scandalous in the academy.

The remainder of *The Witch in History* is less speculative. Purkiss suggests that in any era, historians define witches as "the Other." Whatever a witch is, the historian is not. Witches are poor, uneducated, and female; the historian is well-off, well-educated, and male. Witches are credulous, prejudiced, and primitive; the historian is skeptical, open-minded, and civilized. It is quite true that this formulation works for Robin Briggs—but, except for her gender, it seems equally to apply to Diane Purkiss.

More interestingly, Purkiss suggests that women in early modern Europe also saw the witch as "the Other." The witch was "a kind of anti-housewife," who destroyed and blighted rather than created and nourished, and wished ill rather than good to her family. A good housewife was skilled in what can seem a sort of white magic; she turned milk into butter, wool into yarn and cloth, inedible animal and vegetable matter into tasty and nourishing meals, and squalling infants into well-behaved, hardworking children. This was the front on which the witch attacked, and her black magic was blamed when butter did not come, yarn tangled, milk went sour, and babies and children sickened and died. Purkiss suggests that the witch "acts as a metaphor for the experience of watching a child's illness and being able to do nothing as it suffers, an agonizingly common experience for early modern families."

Occasionally Purkiss, like Briggs, proposes that the psychological mechanism of projection was at work in some witchcraft cases: that the witch was accused of doing what the mother unconsciously wanted to do in moments of exasperation. This seems possible; after all, what housewife hasn't sometimes wanted to set a burnt supper before a grumpy husband? She also remarks that "stories of child bewitchment express and manage mothers' fears that their children will not love them or will reject them" and "reveal deeper fears of children themselves...." In early modern Europe, children who behaved very badly could be said to be bewitched or possessed, thus relieving their parents of guilt—a ploy that has also been used occasionally by fundamentalists in contemporary America.

Purkiss suggests that the witch also disrupted the boundaries between the home and the world, entering her neighbor's house when not invited, refusing to return borrowed tools, and sometimes leaving unwanted and dangerous objects like knives and hammers in magically dangerous places, such as "near the threshold or in bedstraw." At other times, the witch was seen as wanting to invade the home and take over the role of the victim as housewife or mother.

Though the witch trials ended in the early eighteenth century, Purkiss says, faith in the existence of witches did not. "Nineteenth- and twentieth-century folklorists record numerous stories and beliefs . . . which exactly parallel the tropes, narratives, and ideas" found in the classic trial depositions. This remains true: not so long ago I heard a friend who was seriously ill ask that a certain acquaintance not be admitted to her house. "I always feel worse after she's been here," my friend said, only partly joking, "and I think those wheat-germ cookies she brought last time made me sick. I'm sure she's a witch, really."

Like my friend, Diane Purkiss seems at times to believe in the supernatural. She criticizes Reginald Scot's famous skeptical treatise, *The Discoverie of Witchcraft*, saying that it "begins the long process of recuperating women's supernatural power as hysteria and madness," though she adds in a footnote that Scot also explained witchcraft as everyday trickery. For Scot, real witchcraft was impossible because God would not allow it; he could not possibly "be made obedient and servile to obey and perform the will and commandment of a malicious old witch." But in Purkiss's opinion, even modern analyses of witch stories have a fatal drawback: "They cannot admit the possibility that the supernatural might actually exist."

Like many poststructuralist writers, Diane Purkiss is much involved with ideas about what is called "the body." Somewhat confusingly she proposes that the witch (who, for her, is always female) represents "a very specific fantasy about the female body. . . . [She] is a fantasy-image of the huge, controlling, scattered, polluted, leaky . . . maternal body of the Imaginary." This female body, even if formless and shapeless, may be (as others have suggested) a metaphor for the house. One familiar example of this equivalence is the magic house made of bread or gingerbread in "Hansel and Gretel," which according to Purkiss, "embodies and represents" the witch's magical power. Like many other commentators, she remarks that the witch is the bad mother who wishes to eat children rather than feed them. In modern versions, she points out, the house is often made of candy and cake instead of bread, and the lost children are no longer eating from need, but gorge themselves on food which would normally be rationed by caring parents. . . . The witch becomes the modern idea of a "bad mother," a greedy consumer who sacrifices children to her own needs and fails to discipline their oral cravings so that they become as monstrously greedy as she is.

Purkiss also discusses the witch's familiar, which she sees as a kind of demon child, suckled by the witch with blood rather than milk. As she says, this identification made sense in the sixteenth and seventeenth centuries, when breastfeeding was more dangerous than it is today, not only because of the possibility of infections but because if a woman's diet was poor, feeding a child could weaken her seriously. (Even today many nursing mothers develop cavities if they don't get enough calcium—as I and several of my friends did.) Some familiars were affectionate and helpful; others were difficult or unreliable. "Joan Upney's familiars proved . . . unsatisfactory: her mole pined away and died, and her replacement toads kept abandoning her for other people"—exactly like real children, who tend to marry and move away.

Purkiss, like Robin Briggs, notes that the identity of witch was usually imposed from without rather than chosen, and most people refused it at first. Even after legal accusation arid torture, many died protesting their innocence. A few, however, accepted the role of witch sooner, sometimes even without being accused. Apart from the danger of a trial, this role had certain advantages. Claiming to be a witch or a cunning woman could change your social status and give you the sort of power few poor peasants had. The same process of choice can be observed in nineteenth-century spiritualist circles, where lower-middle-class women who successfully claimed to communicate with the spirit world could not only evade the Victorian rules for proper self-effacing, homebound female behavior, but might achieve unexpected fame and fortune, as Verena Tarrant does—though only for a while—in Henry James's *The Bostonians*.

PEOPLE

Archie's Gifts

A. R. Ammons, known to most people who ever met him as Archie, was an apparently simple, but in fact complicated and sometimes difficult, person and poet. He could be friendly and interested in people, especially his students; he could also be cool, detached, and at times unfriendly and uninterested in anyone. To hear him talk about writers whose work he liked was often exciting and even inspiring; but he could be cruel and dismissive of those he did not admire. He could be generous, again especially to his students, but he could also on occasion be resentful and even vengeful, refusing to allow certain poets to be invited to teach or even read at Cornell. But we do not ask that a great writer should be a consistently good man; that is not why we value him.

The outward simplicity and modesty of Archie's verse disguised both great ambition and an ambitious and complex seriousness. Even his earliest poems celebrated the minute and glorious details of the natural world, and also, incidentally, his own gifts of patient observation and dazzling representation. In "Bees Stopped," for instance, he calls attention to some of the small things that "people never see" but that the poet himself looks at closely enough to rejoice in:

> Bees stopped on the rock
> and rubbed their headparts and wings
> rested then flew on:
> ants ran over the whitish greenish reddish
> plants that grow flat on rocks
> and people never see
> because nothing should grow on rocks:

Many readers of this poem, the next time they were outdoors, will have looked more carefully at the life that is everywhere around them, and really seen (perhaps for the first time) bees resting and rubbing their wings, and the plants that grow flat on rocks—I know I did. And then, like Archie, they went on whistling—and by implication, rejoicing.

Even Archie's shortest poems often contain significant messages, in astonishingly condensed form.

> The reeds give
> way to the
> wind and give
> the wind away

Here he reminds us to look carefully at how reeds move before a wind, and how by this movement they reveal the invisible presence of the wind. But, as most readers know, in classical mythology it was reeds out of which Pan made his pipes, the traditional instrument of the poet. The reeds in this poem "give way to the wind"—that is, they are weaker than it is. But they can also reveal its presence, and they can give it a voice.

Moreover, the very existence of this brief verse reminds us that Archie, though now, alas, invisible to all who loved and admired him—is still present. His poems, in yet another sense of the phrase "give away," are his gift of himself to us.

Barbara Epstein

The day we met, Barbara Zimmerman, as she was then, was sitting in the Radcliffe College cafeteria in Agassiz Hall with a cup of black coffee. She was also chain smoking, as she was to do, fatally, for the rest of her life. She was slight and pale and pretty, with soft brown untidy hair and a sudden wide bright smile. Her black turtleneck jersey and stack of books not on any assigned list instantly marked her out as what would presently be called a beatnik. Almost at once I was amazed by her low-key but scarily observant comments on these books, and on some of the other girls sitting nearby, with their tight perms and twinsets, matching lipstick and nail polish, and matching minds. She was a freshman, only sixteen years old, and her nickname at the time was Bubsey, so how did she know so much? It was a question many people were to ask over the next sixty years.

Barbara's quiet, often almost invisible brilliance was all the more striking because she had started life with real disadvantages. She had a scholarship to Radcliffe, but she could not afford to stay in a dorm; instead she commuted to college from her parents' small row house in Brighton. Barbara also been born without a left hand, and she once told me that her parents thought at first that they would have to put her in an institution. After she turned out to be extremely intelligent, their highest hope was that she might become a teacher of other disabled children. All her life, her way of dealing with her disability was to act as if it did not exist, and everyone who knew and admired her followed her lead. They opened doors for her and carried bags of groceries or books, without saying anything or asking if they could help. I also had been a damaged child, and we once agreed that our problems were not, as some people seemed to assume, a melodramatic tragedy, but "just a great big lifelong drag."

After graduating from Radcliffe with honors, Barbara moved to New York, just as I and many of our friends did. But opportunities for young women who couldn't type or file and had no family connections were rare. It took her nearly a year to find a full-time job, and only unusual courage and determination kept her looking. This courage was visible again at the end of her life when, exhausted, and knowing how ill she was, she continued working until two weeks before her death and came to the American Academy to accept a lifetime award for Service to the Arts (shared with Robert Silvers).

Early in her career Barbara worked as an almost unpaid intern at *Partisan Review*, and then at Random House, where she met the young editor Jason Epstein, whom she was to marry. They had two intelligent and attractive children,

Jacob, now a Los Angeles film producer and screenwriter, and Helen, a molecular biologist specializing in public health in developing countries. But even as a mother Barbara kept on working, now with Edward Gorey at the famous reprint series *The Looking Glass Library*, which revolutionized paperback publishing by making it both respectable and profitable to reprint literary classics.

The job Barbara was most famous for, of course, was as coeditor, with Robert Silvers, of *The New York Review of Books*. Founded during the New York newspaper strike of 1963, as what at first looked like a temporary replacement for the *New York Times Book Review*, the *NYRB* went on to become probably the most famous literary magazine in the English-speaking world. It changed serious reporting on the arts and politics and science and society by giving writers both the space and the time to say all they wanted to say, and expert help in saying it as well as possible. The *NYRB* was especially well known for finding writers who were not already well known themselves, many of them from other countries, and encouraging them to propose subjects for reviews and essays, rather than simply assigning currently prominent authors to currently popular topics. One result of all this was a long list of good books that began as *NYRB* articles, many of which probably would not have existed otherwise.

Barbara's editorial skill and her editorial tact were remarkable. Her first response to a manuscript was always enthusiastic; but when the proofs arrived, the margins would be full of questions and suggestions and sometimes embarrassing corrections. Often there would be three or four sets of proofs, and I sometimes felt awkward when I received congratulations on one of my articles, since I knew how much its apparently easy style and accuracy of detail were owing to her. Many other writers have said the same, commenting on how much time Barbara had spent on their pieces, and how reluctant she was to take credit for her contribution to them.

Because Barbara was so kind, generous, and modest—she never gave speeches, interrupted anyone, or raised her voice—it was easy to underestimate how much she knew and saw. There seemed to be nothing she hadn't read, and no one she'd never known or seen—and sometimes seen through. Her accounts of public occasions were often brilliantly comic: I remember how she described Norman Mailer standing on the bottom step of a staircase to lecture George Plimpton and several other men, all of whom were considerably taller than he, on the errors of the current administration. Offered a drink, Mailer seemed eager, but he refused to step down to get it; instead he insisted it be passed to him by his audience.

Barbara gave wonderful parties, successfully mixing unmatching guests: conservatives and radicals, young and old, provincial and international, famous and unknown. Some of the best parties took place during the last seventeen years of her life, which she shared with the gifted journalist Murray Kempton. Like him, she loved a good personal or political scandal, and often somehow knew it before the newspapers did. At the same time, she was strikingly discreet. You knew that nothing you told her would ever be repeated, and also that she would never tell you anything about anyone that you didn't know already. Sometimes I thought that Barbara carried this rule too far. Occasionally she would say with a sigh of regret that she couldn't meet me that evening because she had to "go to something." It would then turn out that "something" was a party given by people we both knew well, and to which I had also been invited. In the same way, she was more likely to conceal than to reveal her close acquaintance with anyone, especially if they were in any way famous.

It was always a wonder to me how Barbara managed to read so much, including, apparently, most of the books discussed in her magazine. When I asked her about this once, she simply said, "I read enough." In any case, she read enough of a great many books to produce some amazingly perceptive and original remarks about them. One of my great regrets is that I never wrote any of these comments down. Another, more serious, is that Barbara never published anything herself, as far as I know, though for a long time I hoped a manuscript or a diary would turn up. Now and then I would suggest that she should write her memoirs. Her reply was always, "Oh, I couldn't do that." Just as well, maybe—the world must still be full of people who are not only grieving for her loss, but sighing with relief that some comic incident in their lives may never be revealed.

It is hard for me, even now, to realize that if I were to go to 33 West 67th Street and take the antique elevator to apartment 3F, where I so often stayed, Barbara would not be there. Without her, the building, once so important in my life, is meaningless; the whole world, and especially New York, seems darker, sadder, and most of all, less interesting.

Edward Gorey

I met him, very appropriately, in a bookstore named after a legendary plant with magical uses: the Mandrake Bookshop on Mount Auburn Street in Cambridge, Massachusetts. It was the sort of shop you seldom see now: cozy and cluttered, with free coffee. You could browse the shelves, or sit and read on the big sagging sofa, without anyone asking "Can I help you?" which of course always translates as, "All right, buy something or scram." Not everyone did, but the bookshop managed to keep going, because back then—over sixty years ago now—rents were not that expensive, and neither were books.

Ted Gorey often hung out at the Mandrake. He was a friend of the owner, Helen McCormick, who was only a couple of years older than us. Ted was twenty-five when we met, just back from two years as an Army typist, finishing up college on the G.I. Bill. He wasn't the striking figure he later became. He looked like a pale lanky engineering student, unstylishly dressed and unremarkable except for his height. He had a crewcut and no facial hair; he wore T-shirts and jeans and sneakers, and when it was cold, a black turtleneck sweater. I was twenty-three, already graduated and working as an editorial assistant in Boston.

We began talking and discovered we liked the same books; the only difference was that Ted had already read almost all my favorites, and I hadn't heard of many of his. After a while we began to meet on purpose, and to go to museums and films together, usually without my husband, Jonathan Bishop, who was working too hard. He wanted to become a professor of English—and he did become a professor—but this meant that he had to do very well in school and didn't have much free time for anything else.

Jonathan and I were living in a one-room apartment on Harvard Street, and if people were there talking, he couldn't study, so Ted and I would usually meet at the Mandrake or at a coffee shop. When the warm weather came, we began going for walks around Cambridge, and one day we went to the old graveyard near Harvard Square. The tombstones there are strange and wonderful, but time and weather were blurring them and wearing them down. We wanted to save them somehow, and so we began making tombstone rubbings. It's easy to do: you take a big piece of shelf paper, stick it to the tombstone with tape, and rub over it with the flat side of a wax crayon in any color you like. If you want a more brilliant effect, when you get home you go over the paper with a sponge soaked in black or colored ink. In those days there were no felt-tip pens, but you could buy many different colors of ink almost anywhere.

Later on we began driving to other graveyards in Boston

and its suburbs, and finding many more strange tombstones. I don't know if any of Ted's original rubbings have survived—mine are all gone, and I regret this very much. But in many of his books, as well as his titles for the TV show *Masterpiece Theatre*, you can see their influence—that of both the nineteenth-century tombstones with their urns and weeping willows, and the earlier ones with their winged cherubs and angels and skulls and crossbones, strange fruits and flowers, and the circular patterns that look like Celtic crosses or magical symbols. Ted preferred the older tombstones, and their strange inscriptions and scary verses. One that we often came across read:

> Behold and think as you pass by,
> As you are now, so once was I.
> As I am now, so you will be.
> Prepare to die and follow me.

It was on one of these trips that I realized for the first time that I was not going to live forever. Of course I knew this theoretically, but I hadn't taken it personally. We were in a beautiful graveyard in Concord, Massachusetts, on a warm soft bright summer day, and I said to Ted, "If I die, I want to be buried somewhere like this." And he said, "What do you mean, if you die?"

In 1950 both Ted and I became involved in the Poets' Theatre of Cambridge. I worked on costumes and makeup, mostly. Ted designed almost all the posters and programs, and helped to create its distinctive style. He was also one of the sanest and calmest people in an organization that wasn't always calm or even sane, though it was always a lot of fun; I've written about it in a memoir of V. R. Lang, the poet who was one of its founders. Eventually both Ted and I wrote short plays for the theater; his was called *Amabel, or The Partition of Poland*, and was semi-surrealist.

After Ted graduated from Harvard, he got a job with a book publisher in Boston, near Copley Square. I was working in Copley Square too, in the Rare Book Room of the Boston Public Library. It wasn't all fun: Ted spent a lot of time packing and shipping books and taking them to the post office, and I had to dust and shelve heavy old volumes of maps and documents and fend off the occasional groping and patting hands of our boss. (Back then nobody complained of this sort of thing, but we took precautions; "If Mr. H asks you to come into his office, stay on the other side of his desk, and excuse yourself if you need to," I was warned my first week on the job.)

We were both also badly paid, but our jobs had compensations: we got first look at a lot of books and we could meet regularly. We used to have lunch or an early supper together in a cafeteria on Marlborough Street; I still remember the two sausages with sauerkraut and applesauce that was one of the cheapest items on the menu. From 1949 to 1952, when Ted moved to New York, we saw more of each other than of anyone else—we were best friends.

Ted then was already the person he later became famous as: immensely intelligent, perceptive, amusing, inventive, skeptical, and a scarily gifted artist. He saw through anyone who was phony, or pretentious, or out for personal gain, very fast. As he said very early in our friendship, in September 1951, according to my journal, "I pity any opportunist who thinks I'm an opportunity." Ted had crushes on acquaintances sometimes, mostly older men, but nothing much ever came of them, and I think he preferred it that way. Later in life he told an interviewer that he had never been romantic, and was not really interested in sex. I also noticed quite soon that he did not much like to be touched, and respected this almost unconsciously.

In 1953 Ted moved to New York City. At first he didn't care much for the place. Here's an excerpt from a letter he wrote me that September:

> All the brilliant thoughts and such which I had about New York seem to have vanished or shriveled by this time, and it's just another place, with better bookstores, and more movies to go to.... Though when the weather is really good, it does seem to have a clarity and glitter I never saw anywhere else. I feel like a captive balloon, motionless between sky and earth. I want birds to bring me messages.

Over the following years Ted gradually grew to love the city, especially after he discovered the New York City Ballet. He became a co-director of the Looking Glass Press, which reprinted lost literary classics, almost all of them with his brilliant cover designs and illustrations. He also began to be noticed not only for his strange but fascinating small books with titles like *The Wuggly Ump* and *The Sinking Spell*, but for his whimsical and memorable cover illustrations for *The New York Review*, and the serial he contributed to its pages, "Les Mysteres de Constantinople, whose heroine was thought by many people to resemble one of the *NYRB*'s coeditors, Barbara Epstein.

Personally Ted was always somewhat noticeable because he was so tall and thin, but now he began to attract more attention. He dressed more and more eccentrically; he grew a mustache and wore a lot of heavy, strange rings. People started to turn around to look at him on the street. After a while he grew a beard too; he began wearing fur coats with his white sneakers, and sometimes the coat matched the beard. Eventually he became both a famous artist and writer and a famous New York character, often recognized in public. People approached him in restaurants or went up to him at intermission at the ballet to say how much they admired his work. He had many friends, but he continued to live alone and remained physically detached from other human beings.

For many years he continued to enjoy New York life. Besides the New York City Ballet, his other enthusiasms were classical art, Victorian novels, silent films, all of which provided inspiration for his work. His passion for the productions of George Balanchine and the principal dancer Suzanne Farrell was so great that at one time he attended every performance. After Balanchine's death he lost interest in dance and also, eventually, in the city. In 1983 he moved with his cats to Cape Cod, where he had already spent many summers, and had a large extended family and many friends.

To enter the world of Edward Gorey is to step into a kind of parallel Gothic universe full of haunted mansions, strange topiary, and equally haunted and strange beings. Though they are mainly well-meaning and well-dressed and live in surroundings of slightly decaying Victorian and Edwardian luxury, they tend to seem lost, baffled, or oppressed by life. They play croquet and go on picnics and have elaborate tea parties, but somehow things often go wrong. There are sudden deaths and disappearances, and the human characters are often haunted, not only by ghosts but by strange creatures of all sorts, some of which resemble giant bugs, while others suggest hairy wombats or small flying lizards or devils.

In many of his books, children especially are at risk. They fall victim to natural disasters, are carried off by giant birds or eaten by comic monsters like the *Wuggly Ump*. In *The Gashly-*

crumb Tinies every letter of the alphabet announces the death of a little girl or boy. Yet somehow the overall effect is not tragic, but merely strange and mysterious, just as it often is in the work of Edward Lear, whom Gorey greatly admired.

In these macabre comedies almost no one looks happy— with the striking exception of the cats, who always seem to be contented and pleased with themselves. Often they appear to be having a wonderful time, especially on the covers of the anthologies of Gorey's work, *Amphigorey* and *Amphigorey Too*.

Of course, in real life Edward Gorey was remarkably fond of cats. According to report, after he moved to New York he seldom had less than five at any one time, and when I visited his apartment in Manhattan I had the impression that there were at least seven or eight in residence, all of them looking extremely well cared for and well fed, even smug. As long as Ted was not working the cats were allowed to use him as a sort of soft furniture, and sometimes several might be purring on his lap—but I have also heard him swear and seen him drop a cat or two abruptly off his drawing board onto the floor.

Though Ted always denied being inspired by real life, I have sometimes thought that two of his early books were partly a comment on my inexplicable (to him) decision to reproduce. In 1953, when the result of this decision, my son John, was about six months old, I wrote Ted a note that said, "I can't go to the movies because I have to stay home to take care of the beastly baby," and enclosed a perhaps not very flattering photo of John. Ted replied, on September 10:

Thank you so much for the picture of your infant. As it happened, as it always seems to, which is sometimes boring and sometimes not, I got into a kind of flap over the weekend, and wrote and illustrated a book which I am dedicating to aforementioned infant. It is apparently very odd indeed . . . when I took it to show Cap [EG's editor], he behaved most nervously, and kept looking at me as if he had never seen me before; he even dragged out a bottle and gave me a drink, this being eleven o'clock in the morning. He is brooding over it at present, but intimated that in ten years perhaps the public would be ready for it. . . . The title of it is The Beastly Baby and that is really all I can tell you about it except that it is a sort of depraved cautionary tale with no moral at all.

The baby Ted created is indeed beastly, and comes to a very bad end. As for the book, it was not published for nearly ten years. After it eventually became available, in 1962, I would sometimes give a copy to friends whose babies were behaving especially badly; I think the message was that things could be a lot worse than they were.

The Doubtful Guest, which was dedicated to me under my married name at the time, Alison Bishop, appeared in 1957. It recalls a remark I made to Ted when John was less than two years old. I said that having a young child around all the time was like having a houseguest who never said anything and never left. This, of course, is what happens in the story. The Doubtful Guest appears out of nowhere. It is smaller than anyone else; it has "a peculiar appearance" at first and does not understand language. As time passes. it becomes greedy and destructive: it tears pages out of books, has temper tantrums, and walks in its sleep. Yet nobody even tries to get rid of the creature. It is just always there. It sits around, or moves from room to room, and it always wears sneakers. The attitude of the other characters towards it remains one of resigned acceptance.

Who is this Doubtful Guest? The last page of the story makes everything clear:

It came seventeen years ago—and to this day
It has shown no intention of going away.

Of course, after about seventeen years most children leave home. The Doubtful Guest is a child, and since the book was published many mothers have recognized this. My own doubtful guest left home at eighteen, and is now over sixty. He still comes to visit, but he always has plenty to say, and often I think he leaves too soon, so there is hope for anyone who has this kind of guest in their own home right now. I myself still have a version of the original one, because one of my daughters-in-law who was a Gorey fan made me a stuffed Doubtful Guest, which still sits in a Victorian armchair in our spare bedroom.

Another book of Edward Gorey's that I was perhaps somewhat involved with was *The Curious Sofa*, a pornographic work, which was published in 1961. When I worked in the Rare Book Room at the Boston Public Library, there was a locked stack full of old-fashioned, not always very hard-core erotica, and when nobody in authority was around, it was possible for me and/or a visitor like Ted to look at these books. I think that they were perhaps one source of *The Curious Sofa*, which isn't pornographic at all, but makes fun of the genre. At the time there was still a lot of complaint in the press about so-called dirty writing, which Ted regarded as rather silly. Here are the captions of the first two pages of his parody, both with perfectly respectable illustrations:

Alice was eating grapes in the park, when Herbert, an extremely well-endowed young man, introduced himself to her.
He invited her to go for a ride in a taxi-cab, on the floor of which they did something Alice had never done before.

The Curious Sofa continues like this throughout, continually suggestive but never in the slightest way explicit. Some people thought that its heroine was based on me, because she has a similar name and rather resembles me as I was then. (I've still got the same haircut.) Even a few of our friends assumed that I was Alice, and I had to work hard to convince them that I hadn't had any of the experiences that she seems perhaps to have had.

Nobody I know of has ever complained that *The Curious Sofa* should be banned. But a few readers have claimed that many of Edward Gorey's books are too frightening for children; that kids shouldn't be allowed to see them. People even say that Ted hated children. None of this is true. In spite of the remarkable amount of infanticide in his work, he was very nice to my three sons, and they liked him and loved his books. I have a wonderful photograph of Ted playing with my youngest son, both of them equally intent on the castle they are building. After *The Beastly Baby* was finally published, I wrote him a postcard, thanking him for sending me a copy. It reads:

> The boys love it. Yesterday they were running around, pointing their toy guns at each other saying "I'm the beastly baby and I'm shooting up the bric-a-brac." So I want you to know that there is one family in the world in which your books are just as much a beloved part of childhood as Beatrix Potter.

Moreover, in spite of what some critics think of as the possible sinister or anxiety-producing effect of Edward Gorey's books on children, all mine turned out just fine.

In Ted's books, it must be admitted, there is often a kind of gray darkness, in which death is met with indifference; it is just what happens. Not so in real life. When Gorey died, the website maintained by his fans (goreography.com) recorded scores of messages of shock, grief, and passionate admiration from correspondents all over the world, aged thirteen to eighty. Many described their surprise and joy when they first saw Gorey's work, and declared that they had found friends and lovers through a mutual enthusiasm for his work; others said that they had rejected acquaintances who didn't like it.

The loss of Edward Gorey is the loss not only of a brilliant and original writer and artist, but a gifted stage and costume designer. He has also taken with him many other greatly talented imaginary people, including Ogdred Weary, author of *The Curious Sofa*, E. G. Deadworry, author of *The Awdrey-Gore Legacy*, Mrs. Regera Dowdy, author of *The Pious Infant* and translator of Eduard Blutig's *The Evil Garden*. (Evidently these writers, and many others, are pseudonyms—and in some cases anagrams—of "Edward Gorey"; though if we accept this, we must also accept the astounding fact that Mr. Gorey produced over a hundred books.) But we must not despair. Often the characters in Gorey's work who die or disappear leave only a void behind: empty crosshatched streets and withered formal gardens and rooms with peculiar wallpaper. We are luckier; we have his books.

James Merrill

I t is rare for those born with great talent and great wealth
neither ostentatiously to display either one, nor to coast on
these golden flying carpets of advantage. James Merrill did
neither. He lived modestly, and all his life he almost invisibly
shared his fortune with less fortunate artists and writers, most
notably through the Ingram Merrill Foundation—the name
of which reunited his long-divorced and estranged parents,
Helen Ingram and the Wall Street tycoon Charles Merrill.
There were also many individual gifts, one of which under-
wrote the publication of my first book, a memoir of a friend.

It wasn't only financial support that Jimmy Merrill and
his partner David Jackson gave: they were also amazingly
generous with their time, attention, and affection. For many
years, whenever I thought I had finished a manuscript, I
showed it to them, and many of my books were saved by their
tactful comments from a fate worse than publication.

In the same way, Jimmy did not use his literary gifts

to trumpet their own brilliance. On first reading, his work often seemed unassuming even casual; only gradually did its wit, invention, and serious engagement with both the world around him and the poetic tradition appear. Even in his autobiography and in the dramatic Sandover poems, he gave "JM" no special privileges, but turned his cool, amused, sometimes frighteningly penetrating gaze on himself as well as on the world around him. His attitude towards "real life" and world news was the same. Everything, even the most obscure news item or the slightest flicker of a match or a joke, might be serious—yet nothing was solemn.

In the last chapter of his memoir of his early years, *A Different Person*, James Merrill speaks of his love affair with certain words. The affectionate, detailed consideration he brings to the subject would not surprise anyone who knew how intensely aware he was of language, even in the most casual and banal circumstances. Sometimes when I was with him, I would hear a cliché hop out of my mouth, like the toads and snakes that afflict the bad sister in the fairy tale. Most of the time he would just slightly wince, but now and then he would scrutinize the cliché with a herpetologist's care and detachment.

For instance, when I described my ten-year-old son's state of mind by saying that he was "As mad as a wet hen," Jimmy's response was "Yes. I wonder, would the juvenile equivalent be 'as mad as a wet chicken'? Or perhaps one could use the masculine form, 'as mad as a wet cock.'"

Almost every time I spoke to Jimmy, or read something he had written—whether it was a poem or a postcard—I was reminded that it is the job not only of a writer, but also of every living person, to take language both lightly and seriously, as he did—often at the same time; he must be one of the few writers who could successfully use words like "asymmetries," "X-ray-wise," and "oops!" in the same poem. In his work the flattest clichés are transformed into glowing images, and worn-out puns and similes expand and come alive. And almost always, behind the flash and shimmer of his language, there are deeper meanings.

In the black light of his death, many of his lines reverberate even more. At one point he published a wonderful travel essay, "Japan: Prose of Departure," a travelogue that flows effort-lessly into and out of a series of haiku and thoughts about a dying friend in New York. In the poem "Prose of Departure," he remarks that the clinic where his friend is dying is "vast and complex as an ocean liner." He goes on to speak of the passengers, "all in the same boat . . . each of them visibly

> at sea. Yes, yes, these
> old folks grown unpresuming,
> almost Japanese,
>
> had embarked too soon
> —Bon voyage! Write!—upon their
> final honeymoon.

Later he describes a visit to a Noh theater, where an actor plays the parts successively of a maiden pearl-diver, her mother's ghost, and a dancing dragon. The performer is

> a middle-aged man—
> but time, gender, self are laws
> waived by his gold fan.

A pearl-diver, a benevolent ghost, and a dancing dragon; that sounds about right. Bon voyage! I miss you all terribly.

CHILDREN'S BOOKS

The Good Bad Boy: Pinocchio

Today many people think they know all about Pinocchio. They believe that he is a wooden marionette who becomes a human boy; that he was swallowed by a huge fish; and that whenever he told lies his nose grew longer. (As a result of this last occurrence, for over a hundred years politicians have been caricatured with a lengthened nose when they prevaricate in public—especially Richard Nixon, who already had a kind of Pinocchio nose.)

These people are right, but often only in a very limited way. They know Pinocchio only from the sentimentalized and simplified Disney cartoon, or the condensed versions of his story that are thought more suitable for children. The original novel by Carlo Collodi, which today survives mainly in scholarly editions, is much longer, far more complex and interesting, and also much darker. The critic Glauco Cambon has called it one of the three most influential works in Italian literature (the others, he claims, are Dante's *Divine Comedy* and Manzoni's *The Betrothed*). For him, and those who know the real version, *The Adventures of Pinocchio* is not an amusing, light-hearted fantasy, but a serious fable about art and life. It is a story about growing up—and it is also, in essential ways, a story about growing up poor and Italian.

Carlo Collodi, whose real name was Carlo Lorenzi, was born in Florence in 1826, the first of ten children of household servants. When he did well in the local school, his parents' employer paid for his further education in the hope that he would become a priest. This did not happen. Instead, after graduation Lorenzi went to work for a bookseller, and eventually became a liberal journalist, skeptical of both education and the church. In *Pinocchio,* school is something that all boys dread, and religion is hardly mentioned.

Originally Pinocchio was published as a serial in the newspaper *Il gionale per i bambini* (The paper for children). It appeared in eight parts between July and October of 1881, and then in eleven more installments from February 1882 to January 1883. The form of the story was that of a picaresque novel, in which, perhaps because of the pressures of time, some of the chapters are more original and/or better integrated into the story than others. Several of these episodes— for example those in which Pinocchio meets a giant serpent, is caught in a trap and made to serve as a watchdog, rides on the back of a pigeon, and is mistaken for a fish by a monstrous green-haired fisherman—are often left out of the condensed English-language versions.

The Disney film omits even more of the story, and changes it drastically. Geppetto, Pinocchio's foster father, appears to be a prosperous toy maker, and the town where he lives looks Swiss or Bavarian: his workshop is full of music boxes and cuckoo clocks. In the original story, however, Geppetto is a desperately poor Italian woodcarver. When the film begins, Pinocchio is merely a wooden toy; he comes to life only when a fairy grants Geppetto's wish for a child. In the book, Pinocchio is alive from the start. Though he is only a nameless stick of firewood in the shop of the carpenter Master Anthony, he can already speak and move. When Master Anthony strikes the stick with his axe, it cries out "Ouch! You hurt me!" The carpenter is terrified, and offers the piece of wood to his friend Geppetto, who wants to make a marionette. It continues to act up, mocking Geppetto and striking Master Anthony, provoking two fist-fights between the old friends.

When Geppetto gets home, he begins to carve the mario-nette. But as soon as Pinocchio's mouth is finished he laughs at Geppetto and sticks out his tongue, and once he has arms, he snatches Geppetto's wig off his head. When his legs and feet are finished, he runs away.

From the start, Collodi's Pinocchio is not only more self-conscious but far less simple than the cute little toy boy of the cartoon. He is not only naïve, but impulsive, rude, selfish, and violent. In theological terms, he begins life in a state of original sin; while from a psychologist's point of view, he represents the amoral, self-centered small child, all uncensored id.

Unable to control his own impulses, Pinocchio provokes external control. As he runs down the street, pursued by Geppetto, he is stopped by a policeman, who returns him to his foster father. Immediately, in a maneuver that will be familiar to many parents of small children, Pinocchio flings himself on the ground and declares that he won't walk anymore. A crowd gathers and (like some modern experts on child development) begins to blame Geppetto for Pinocchio's delinquency. Eventually they convince the policeman to put Geppetto in prison. In Collodi's world, the law is always stupid and often corrupt. It is usually the victim of a crime, rather than the perpetrator, who is punished. (Later in the story, when Pinocchio goes to court to complain that he has been robbed, the judge, who is a gorilla, sends him rather than the robbers to jail. He is released only when he falsely admits that he is a criminal.)

Once he is free again, Pinocchio returns home, where he meets what many readers have recognized as his conscience, or external superego, in the form of a Talking Cricket. The Cricket scolds Pinocchio for running away, and warns him about the dangers of idleness: if he quits school, he will grow up to be a perfect jackass. But Pinocchio refuses to listen. The only trade in the world that will suit him, he says, is that of "eating, drinking, sleeping, having fun, and living the life of a vagabond from morning to night." When the Cricket remarks that "everyone who follows that trade is bound to end up in the poorhouse or in prison," Pinocchio becomes angry and throws a wooden mallet at the Cricket, killing it. It will appear in the story again, however, first as a mysterious black-clad doctor and finally as a ghost.

Pinocchio's external conscience also appears in the Disney cartoon, but there it has been turned into a comic figure, and rechristened "Jiminy Cricket" (the phrase is, very aptly, an old-fashioned American euphemism for "Jesus Christ"). Jiminy Cricket wears the top hat and tails of a vaudeville performer, he sings and dances, and most of the time his admonitions are amusing but ineffective. Pinocchio only half listens to him, but does him no harm.

Disney's Pinocchio is portrayed as about five or six years old, and throughout the story he remains innocent and simple, like the ideal child of romantic literature. He is without rudeness or malice: what gets him into trouble is curiosity and boredom. Collodi's hero is clearly several years older, and full of aggressive and rebellious impulses which are only tamed at the end of the story. Here he recalls a classic character in American children's fiction of the late nineteenth century, the Good Bad Boy.

This figure made his first important appearance in Thomas Bailey Aldrich's *Story of a Bad Boy* (1869). Aldrich was born and largely grew up in Portsmouth, New Hampshire; he became a popular journalist, poet, and novelist, and later the editor of the *Atlantic Monthly*. His hero, Tom Bailey, who was based on his own childhood self, is "bad" only in contrast to the almost unbelievably pious, obedient, and self-sacrificing little boys and girls who were the protagonists of so many contemporary "moral tales" for children. Tom Bailey has a sense of enterprise and fun. He and his friends occasionally skip school, but they do not become juvenile delinquents. They stage elaborate snowball fights and beat up a local bully. The worst thing they do is to burn an old stagecoach and fire some cannon balls left over from the Civil War. Aldrich's book became very popular, and many imitations followed, including James Otis's *Toby Tyler* (1881), George Wilbur's *Peck's Bad Boy* and his *Pa* (1883), and eventually Booth Tarkington's *Penrod* (1914). But though Toby Tyler runs away from home to join the circus, and the other protagonists are occasionally disobedient or naughty, they are essentially good boys.

The most famous descendant of Aldrich's Tom Bailey, however, is seriously delinquent. This is the eponymous hero of Mark Twain's *Tom Sawyer*, first published in 1876. Tom's boyhood home, Hannibal, Missouri, is closely based on Twain's own hometown of St. Petersburg, and his well-behaved brother and worried mother reappear as Sid and Aunt Polly. Tom is not just adventurous and occasionally naughty. He lies, steals, smokes, skips school, causes an uproar in church, runs away from home, and associates with dubious companions. He loves freedom and pleasure and craves adventure. He is impulsive, thoughtless, and mischievous. At the same time Tom is basically good at heart. He learns from his mistakes, and at the end of the book he is forgiven and reconciled with his family and society. The same thing, of course, happens in Twain's later masterpiece, *Huckleberry Finn* (1884).

Whether or not Collodi read Tom Sawyer, there are similarities between the two stories. But Pinocchio's world is much bleaker than Tom's. Tom's Aunt Polly is by no means rich, but she owns a house with a fenced garden. Pinocchio's foster father, the carpenter Geppetto, is old and seriously poor and must worry constantly about where his next meal is coming from. He lives in a small room under the front steps of a building, with one tiny window, and all he has for furniture is "an old chair, a rickety old bed, and a tumble-down table. A fireplace full of burning logs was painted on the wall opposite the door. Over the fireplace there was painted a pot full of something which kept boiling happily away and sending up clouds of what looked like real steam."

In Geppetto's room, warmth and hot food are mocking two-dimensional illusions.

The St. Petersburg of Mark Twain's childhood was a sometimes violent frontier town. As a boy, Twain saw a man stabbed to death, just as Tom Sawyer does. But Pinocchio's world is even more dangerous; it is full of people who want to exploit and rob and even kill the hero. When Tom and Huck run away from home, they meet both good and bad characters. Pinocchio encounters only hostile humans, and for him even the animal kingdom is dangerous. Though he is helped by a bird and a fish, his most important opponents are animals, two of whom also have parallels in Twain's work. These are the Fox and the Cat, shabby but pretentious con men very reminiscent of the King and the Duke in *Huckleberry Finn* (1884). (Since Pinocchio was not translated into English until 1892, it seems likely that this is just an instance of types familiar since Aesop's Fables reappearing in fiction.) The King and the Duke spend most of their energy on robbing and defrauding strangers, and they do not commit murder. The Fox and the Cat, however, plot to kill Pinocchio for his gold pieces and almost succeed. In both books the con men come to a bad end, but only Huck Finn feels pity for them. When Huck sees the King and the Duke tarred and feathered and run out of town on a rail, he remarks:

> Well, it made me sick to see it; and I was sorry for them poor pitiful rascals, it seemed like I couldn't ever feel any hardness against them any more in the world. It was a dreadful thing to see.

At the end of *Pinocchio*, the hero and his father come across the Fox and the Cat, who once pretended to be blind and lame. Now the Cat is really blind and the Fox sick and almost hairless, and they have become beggars.

> "Oh, Pinocchio," the Fox cried in a tearful voice. "Give us some alms, we beg of you! We are old, tired, and sick."
> "Sick," repeated the Cat.

"If you are poor, you deserve it! Remember the old proverb which says: Stolen money never bears fruit."

And though the Fox and the Cat beg for mercy, all they get from Pinocchio is two more proverbs, after which Pinocchio and Geppetto "calmly went on their way.'" This ending may strike us as harsh, but it is also closer to the pattern of the classic European folk tale, in which villains seldom reform and do not need to be forgiven.

At one point in Tom Sawyer, Tom runs away from home to Jackson's Island in the Mississippi, where he and his friends Huck and Joe can enjoy themselves without interference from adults. They fish, smoke, and pretend to be pirates. But both Tom and Joe are troubled by thoughts of the families they have left behind. They are away only a few days, however, and when they become homesick and return to Hannibal, they are greeted as heroes. The moral seems to be that you can skip school, have a wonderful time camping out, worry and frighten your relatives, and get away with it. When Pinocchio leaves home, on the other hand, he encounters a series of dangers and enemies. A giant snake blocks his path, and when he enters a field to steal grapes, he is caught in a mantrap by a farmer, who uses him as a watchdog to guard his chicken coop.

Pinocchio also travels with other boys to a kind of children's paradise called Funland, where there is no school and "the days go by in play and good times from morning till night." But his holiday lasts far longer than Tom's. He lives in Funland for five months without tiring of it or missing Geppetto. Unlike Tom, he is not troubled by his conscience, or by thoughts of anyone from his former life. Then, as the Talking Cricket has predicted, Pinocchio and his best friend Lampwick gradually turn into jackasses. The first sign of this is that he wakes up one morning with ass's ears. His reaction is violent: "He began to cry, to scream, to knock his head against the wall, but the more he shrieked, the longer and more hairy grew his ears."

When he discovers that the same thing has happened to Lampwick, they begin to laugh, but soon they are fully transformed and can only bray. Then they, with all their comrades, are taken to market and sold by the wicked wagon driver who has lured them to Funland in order to make a profit on their inevitable transformation. Pinocchio goes first to a circus, where he is forced to perform tricks, and is beaten and starved; when he becomes lame, he is sold to a dealer in hides who tries to drown him in order to peddle his skin.

These events are both a metaphor and a warning, one that Collodi reinforces by remarking that "by virtue of playing all the time and never studying, those poor gullible boys turned into so many donkeys." The harsh moral (as true today as it was in Collodi's time) is that poor boys who quit school and hang about doing nothing, playing and enjoying themselves, are likely to end up as exploited and overworked laborers—or possibly dead.

Pinocchio's metamorphoses are frightening, but thematically interesting. During the book he moves from the vegetable to the animal kingdom, rising gradually within each class. His name, which in Tuscany at the time meant "pine nut" or "pine seed"—the contemporary term is *pignolo*—associates him with a plant. He begins life as a featureless stick of firewood (possibly pine wood), which is then transformed into a wooden puppet. Next he moves through animal identities (watchdog and donkey), and finally achieves full human status. Metaphorically, it is the same progression that we see in children, who start out as more or less inert matter, then become ignorant if lovable bundles of need and greed, with short attention spans and a wish to explore the world without regard for its dangers. Like animals, they resist confinement, live in the present, and continually seek food and amusement.

Apart from this possible parallel, why did Collodi chose a marionette for his hero instead of just a naughty boy? Possibly because in the theater what scholars call "performing objects"—puppets, marionettes, automatons, shadow figures, animated props—have advantages denied to human actors. Actors are never the same as the parts they play, and however skilled they may be, we are always aware that there is a real person beneath the disguise. Performing objects, on the other hand, can appear as pure representations of some individual type or character. (For this reason, the British stage designer Gordon Craig once expressed the hope that in the future all actors would be replaced by puppets.)

Pinocchio has sometimes been seen, especially by readers who think first of the Disney version, as a classic fairy tale. If so, it is a tale of a special type. In most fairy stories with a male protagonist, the young hero leaves his original family, has adventures, and ends up marrying a princess and starting a new family. Folklorists refer to such tales as Stories of Adolescence. Pinocchio, by contrast, is what is called a Story of Childhood, like "Jack and the Beanstalk" or "Hansel and Gretel." Here the hero does not start a new family; instead he ends up back home with a beloved and loving parent. The same pattern occurs in another well-known Italian children's classic, Dino Buzzati's *The Bears' Famous Invasion of Sicily*, where the central relationship is also between a father and a son, and one important motive behind King Leander's invasion is to find his lost child,

Tony. (Interestingly, when Tony is discovered, he is working for humans as an entertainer—a kind of puppet.)

In folktales the young hero or heroine is often aided by a supernatural figure: a dwarf, a talking animal, a wise woman, or a fairy godmother. In *Pinocchio* this role is played by the Blue Fairy, whose most distinctive feature is the color of her hair. Blue or green hair is a traditional attribute of supernatural beings; sometimes good or neutral, like the Green Man and Green Children of British folklore, and at other times evil like Bluebeard. In *Pinocchio* the Blue Fairy appears in many guises. At first she is a white-faced little girl who declares that she is dead, but she soon proves able to save Pinocchio from near-death, summoning three doctors to cure him. When they part, she claims to be his older sister. Next she appears as a young working woman who takes Pinocchio home, feeds him cauliflower and cake, and declares that she will be his Mama. Later he sees her as a little she-goat with indigo hair, on a rock in the middle of the sea. Finally, at the end of the story, she appears in a dream as a beautiful fairy who changes him into a real boy.

Collodi, however, seems to refuse the idea that Pinocchio is a romantic fairy tale at the very start of his book.

> Once upon a time, there was . . .
> "A king!" my little readers will say right away. "No, children, you are mistaken. Once upon a time there was a piece of wood. It wasn't expensive wood, just the ordinary kind that we take from a woodpile in the winter and put in the stove . . ."

In other words, his story will be grounded not in a world of high-flown fantasy but in the harsh economic realities of working-class life in Italy in the late nineteenth century. It is a place of constant, grinding poverty, eased only by love and self-sacrifice. Pinocchio begins life as a rebellious, inconsiderate, self-centered little boy who disobeys adults and disregards rules, always with dangerous results. Instead of going to school, for instance, he sells the schoolbook Geppetto has bought him and buys a ticket to the puppet theater. There he is entrapped by the terrifying Puppet-Master and nearly burned alive on a kitchen fire.

Willingness to work and sacrifice himself for others is Pinocchio's eventual salvation. At the theater he escapes death when he impulsively offers himself as a substitute for another doomed puppet, briefly touching the Puppet-Master's heart. His final transformation is the result of his willingness to work long hours at an exhausting job to earn money for his ailing foster father, Geppetto, and then for his supernatural mother, the Blue Fairy.

In the Disney film it is inexperience and bad advice rather than selfishness and disobedience that get Pinocchio into trouble. He is led to the puppet theater by two villains, the Cat and the Fox, who—in a very Hollywood touch—promise him fame and money in a song whose refrain is "It's great to be a celebrity." Of course, in Disney's hands Pinocchio did become a kind of celebrity; he also, in the film version, becomes prosperous. In the original novel this does not happen: Pinocchio merely manages, through hard work, to support his foster father—though in the end the Blue Fairy does transform their shabby room into a comfortable cottage and give him forty golden coins. But the important thing is that he becomes "a proper boy," *un ragazzino per bene*" which in Italian, as the critic Ann Lawson Lucas points out, has a double meaning: Pinocchio is now both a real boy and a good boy.

Will Pinocchio remain a good boy? And, if he does, will

readers continue to care about him? The book is thirty-six chapters long, and only in the last two does he consistently behave well. Delinquency and rebellion are more interesting and more fun to read about than moral perfection. As the critic Lois Kuznets says, "Pinocchio is loved the better for his misdemeanors." In this, he may remind us of other Good Bad Boy heroes, both in fiction and in real life. It is perhaps an especially popular type in Italy, where a grown man with a warm heart, a love of escapades, and impatience with social rules and restrictions is often seen as charming and seductive. If someone like this appears truly (though sometimes only temporarily) sorry for his transgressions, he may be forgiven again and again by his friends and relatives, as repentant sinners are by the Catholic Church.

Pinocchio is an Italian story in several other ways. It is full of Northern Italian landscapes and dishes, such as the red mullet with tomato sauce and tripe à la Parmesan that the Fox and the Cat dine on at the hero's expense. It also embodies the traditional Italian belief that the family is of central importance. You can have a good time with your friends, but you can only really trust your kin. Good parents will sacrifice themselves for their children without a murmur, as Geppetto does when there is nothing to eat in the house but three pears, and he allows Pinocchio thoughtlessly and greedily to devour them all. (This episode, like many others, was eliminated from the Disney film.) Good children will also sacrifice themselves for their parents in a real crisis, as Pinocchio does when he and his father, like Jonah in the Bible, escape from the belly of the Great Shark, and he carries Geppetto out of the sea on his back.

Some critics have noted other parallels between Pinocchio and Christian legend. They have remarked that the hero is the foster son of a carpenter, and that he dies and is resurrected at least three times. (In one of these deaths, he is hung on a tree.) They have also suggested that the Blue Fairy is a version of the Virgin, who in art often wears a blue robe—though Mary's robe is usually sky-blue, while Collodi describes the Fairy's hair as indigo.

To some readers, Pinocchio is a sacrificial victim; others have imagined him as a hero of the rebellious working class, whose escapades defy social rules. Psychologists have seen his escape from the Great Shark as a kind of rebirth, and suggested that his expanding nose tells us that lies are virile. Like most great works of children's literature, Pinocchio lends itself to many and varied interpretations, and it will surely continue to do so in the future.

The Royal Family of Elephants

For over seventy years, Babar has been the most famous elephant in the world—and the most controversial. He has been praised as a benevolent monarch, an ideal parent, and a model of family affection, loyalty, justice, good manners, and civilized living. He has also been damned as a sexist, an elitist, a colonialist, and a racist. It has even been proposed that he deserves to be burned alive: see *Should We Burn Babar?* by Herbert Kohl. Clearly, a figure who arouses such intense and conflicting opinions must be more than just the hero of a children's picture book: he must represent important and sometimes contradictory views of both childhood and society.

The complexity of King Babar's world, and some of its contradictions, are partly the result of the fact that his long life has been chronicled by two different biographers. Babar's history began in Paris in 1931, when the pianist Cécile de Brunhoff invented a bedtime story about a baby elephant for her sons, who were then five and six years old. The next day the boys repeated the tale to their father, the artist Jean de Brunhoff, who was inspired to write it down, expand it, illustrate it, and publish it in 1931 as *The Story of Babar*. Over the next eight years he wrote six more Babar books which, like the first, became immensely popular. When he died in 1937, at the age of thirty-seven, the series lapsed. But seven years later his eldest son Laurent, then only twenty but already becoming known as an artist, took up the story. Since then Laurent de Brunhoff has produced over thirty books about Babar and his family and friends, and six with other protagonists, of whom the most famous is a gentle and elusive little man called Bonhomme who lives at the top of a pink mountain. (Friends of Laurent de Brunhoff, as well as some readers, have felt that there was a personal connection between Bonhomme and his creator, and de Brunhoff admits that he has "a special feeling" for him.)

Babar, of course, both is and is not an elephant. Or rather, he is an elephant only in the sense that the characters in Aesop's and Jean de la Fontaine's Fables are animals. Essentially all of them stand for human types and have the traits that humans, sometimes arbitrarily, have assigned to them. La Fontaine's crow, for example, is vain and easily deceived, though real crows are neither conceited nor foolish. As an elephant, Babar is traditionally strong and wise and has a remarkable memory. He is also naturally large and powerful, unlike many animal heroes of children's picture books, who tend to be smaller than humans. From the start, most original editions of the Babar books have appropriately been supersized, just as Beatrix Potter's tales of rabbits and mice are very small.

Babar is not only both animal and human, he is both a child and an adult. His name makes this clear: it combines the French terms for father (papa) and infant (bébé). Babar was the name of a sixteenth-century Indian king; but Laurent de Brunhoff says his father was probably not aware of this when he began the series. Currently, BaBar is also the name given to an electronic testing program used in laboratories.

One sign of his ambiguous position is that, unlike the other adult elephants in the story, he and his wife, Celeste have very small tusks, even after they marry and become parents. They rule a kingdom, but they also enjoy many childish pleasures, as the British critic Margaret Blount has noted:

> Babar does what most small children would like to do—joins in the adult world on a child's terms, and gets away with it.... He can wear grown-up clothes, ride up and down in the lift, go fishing, drive a car, marry Celeste and become King of the Jungle all because his real self is hidden behind an animal hide and he is neither child nor adult but a bit of both. . . .

Another part of the appeal of the Babar series seems to be that, after the first few books, they are about an ideal happy family in a nearly ideal world. Babar and his family visit distant places and even go to outer space, and sometimes they face trouble or danger; but everything always ends well. Their ideal universe also, very early in the series, becomes timeless. Babar is born, grows up, is educated, marries, becomes king, brings the advantages of civilization to his country, and has three children. After that, time stops. Over fifty years pass, and King Babar and Queen Celeste have a fourth child, but nobody grows any older or dies. Babar's cousin Arthur remains an adolescent, and the children never reach puberty. As Margaret Blount puts it, Babar exists "in a perpetual, infantile middle age."

In classic juvenile literature the protagonist is usually a child who leaves home and family, has adventures, and returns home (*Alice in Wonderland, The Wizard of Oz, Pinocchio, Where the Wild Things Are*). Sometimes there are two or more children (A *Wrinkle in Time, Peter Pan, Mary Poppins*), and occasionally the hero or heroine ends up with a new and better family (*Anne of Green Gables, Harry Potter*). In most of the Babar books, however, the family itself is the protagonist. It is an extended three-generational family, in which Babar's early patroness, the Little Old Lady, and his wise elderly councilor Cornelius, play the part of grandparents. Arthur is the impulsive adolescent cousin, and Zephir the monkey his mischievous friend. Babar goes out into the world alone in the first book, but from then on he is almost always accompanied by family members. Together they go to Paris, to America, on vacation to the seashore or the mountains, on hikes in the country, and to another planet. Sometimes one of the children is the center of the story, but the entire family is almost always present and involved, especially at the inevitable happy ending. In this, of course, the books are closer to the real experience of most of their child readers, which may partly account for their popularity.

The environment of Babar is that of the prosperous, well-educated, art-loving French bourgeoisie. Babar and his family go to the theater and hear concerts of both classical and popular music. They favor upper-class sports: they sail, play tennis, swim and ski, practice yoga, go to the races, and camp and hike in the mountains. Good manners are important, and so are good clothes. Jean de Brunhoff's brother was the editor of French *Vogue* and his brother-in-law a famous fashion journalist, and the costumes of Celeste and her daughters are consistently chic. The first thing Babar does after he is befriended by the Old Lady is to go to a large, apparently expensive department store, where he buys a bright green suit, a derby hat, and shoes. His first gift to his subjects is two sets of apparel each—one for work and one for play. Before they put these outfits on, the elephants walk on all fours; afterwards they stand upright. In *The Travels of Babar* (1932), when Babar and Celeste lose their clothes and are stranded on a reef in the ocean, they also lose their quasi-human identity, and the captain of the ship that rescues them can sell them to a circus.

Babar's is an ideal world, a kind of upper-middle-class French Utopia whose capital is literally a heavenly city—as its name, Celesteville, indicates. Its inhabitants have various occupations, but they only work in the mornings—the afternoons are devoted to sports, recreation, and the arts. They live in identical grass-roofed cottages, except for Babar and the Little Old Lady, who have larger houses at the top of a hill, near public buildings that include a school, a library, a sports complex, and a theater. During the over seventy years since the founding of Celesteville the city has grown considerably: it now includes substantial mansions, skyscrapers, and a large art museum.

Though no one ages in Celesteville, modern inventions and modern attitudes gradually appear. Styles in fashion and car design change; motorbikes, television, helicopters, and hang-gliders become visible, and computers and cell phones are surely on their way. Queen Celeste remains a traditional wife and mother who stays home and devotes herself to her children; her older daughter Flora is at first conventionally feminine, passive, and fearful; but in later books she gradually gains in courage and enterprise. Her younger sister Isabelle is a thoroughly modern little girl, slimmer and more active than Flora. She wears in-line skates, listens to music on a portable device, and is eager to explore the world. Eventually, in *The Rescue of Babar* (1993) she journeys to a strange civilization and helps to free her father from captivity.

As Ann Hildebrand, who has written a recent study of *Babar*, points out, the ambiance of the books is generally Gallic. The illustrations show berets, Citroens, Peugeots, crêperies, and croissants, and the signs on the buildings are in French. Babar and his family visit Paris, a seaside resort that suggests Normandy or Brittany, and a chateau in the Dordogne. Ariel Dorfman, in *The Empire's Old Clothes* (1983) has suggested that the attitude towards childhood in the early Babar books is also typically French. "[U]niversal bliss is assured by grown-up figures who never make mistakes, and are unsusceptible to criticism." For Americans, he believes, childhood is an age for fun and adventures, an end in itself, whereas for the French it is a period of probation. This may be so in the early Babar books, but as time passes (or rather stops), the implied message changes, and in the later books Babar's children and his cousin Arthur enjoy a perpetual happy and adventurous youth.

In the Babar books, the kingdom of the elephants is not the only possible society. Besides the human world, containing recognizable places like Paris, New York, Chicago, and North Africa, there are separate civilizations of birds and monkeys and a planet in outer space whose inhabitants look rather like elephants. All these places have much in common with Celesteville. Their citizens are friendly to strangers; they live in comfortable and attractive dwellings under the care of a benevolent ruler, and they enjoy public events.

In Jean de Brunhoff's *Babar and Zephir* (1936) ,the Republic of the Monkeys is ruled by a President, General Huc. He sports a Napoleonic hat and has a fairly large but not very efficient army whose uniforms suggest those of nineteenth-century France or Italy: his soldiers wear red pants, white jackets, and plumed kepis. The principal city, Monkeyville, is on the sea and in a temperate climate. The monkeys wear fashionable clothes and live in small but comfortable houses hung from trees: they have a railway station, cars, a restaurant, and a hairdresser. On a nearby island there is a collection of strange-looking but essentially harmless "monsters," whose greatest fear is boredom. Zephir manages to entertain them brilliantly, telling stories, dressing as a clown and doing tricks, and playing waltzes and polkas on his violin. The overall impression is of a Mediterranean seaside resort with an offshore island populated by eccentric and demanding tourists.

Laurent de Brunhoff's *Babar's Visit to Bird Island* (1951) portrays a simpler and more rural world. It is a strikingly beautiful and colorful book, and one of the author's favorites: according to him, it was inspired by childhood visits to Cap Ferret, south of Bordeaux. The island is roughly bird-shaped and ruled by a king and queen who resemble crested cockatoos. As in *Babar the King*, the inhabitants all have different and appropriate trades: the pelican, with his large beak, is a postman; the pheasants are tailors; the long-legged flamingo and stork are dancers; the parrot and the peacock are actors; the vulture is a butcher; and chickens manage the dairy. There are no monsters, though at one point Babar's daughter Flora

is threatened by an enormous fish. It is a freer and less organized society than that of the monkeys; entertainment and
the enjoyment of life are foremost, and only Babar and his
family wear clothes. The suggestion is of a small semi-tropical island, with colorful, pleasure-loving inhabitants of many
races, where one can enjoy deep-sea fishing and outdoor banquets.

Twenty years later Laurent de Brunhoff took Babar and
his family to outer space, in *Babar Visits Another Planet* (1972).
This time the elephants were not politely invited, as with Bird
Island and Monkeyville, but kidnapped. They were sucked
into an unmanned rocket ship that took many days to reach
its goal: a strange reddish planet where the ground is soft
and mushy like caramel and all buildings are hung from red
balloons. The inhabitants look like small, thin, pear-shaped
elephants with curly ears; they wear clothes and walk on
their hind legs. Civilization is highly developed, with indoor
swimming pools, an automatic fountain that serves cakes and
soft drinks, and a supermarket/shopping mall with motor-
ized carts. It is a crowded urban culture, with an emphasis on
competition and material goods, and the city has an Oriental
appearance. Babar's children sleep in "little wall niches" that
resemble the mini-hotels in Japanese cities, and the signs in
the supermarket appear to be written in Asian characters. It
is also a highly ordered and homogeneous society: the curly-
eared elephants "speak as with one voice, which sounds like
a clarinet."

The reddish planet is in many ways more alien, and possibly more perilous, than the worlds of the monkeys or the
birds—just as Japan is less familiar to French children than a
French or Italian seaside resort. In Monkeyville and on Bird

Island there was no language barrier, but here Babar cannot understand anyone until the end of the story. And though the curly-eared elephants are friendly and hospitable at first, they become very upset when Arthur accidentally breaks one of their red balloons, and Babar and his family are advised to return to Earth immediately to avoid danger.

The most interesting, though least agreeable, alternative society in the Babar books is that of the rhinos. It also, unlike the other alien worlds, appears many times. The rhinos' territory borders that of the elephants, but though they are Babar's neighbors, they are often opposed to him. They are large, clumsy, and subject to fits of aggression and impulsive greed. They have bad manners and no apparent interest in art or music. When they first appear, they, like most of the elephants, walk on four legs and do not wear clothes, but later they, too, appear to have become civilized. They have very bad taste, however: they like vulgar patterns and silly hats. Their king, Rataxes, wears loud-print suits and comic-opera uniforms.

The city of the rhinos is a large metropolis, with square brutalist public buildings that seem to be constructed of gray cement in a semi-Egyptian style. There are no flower gardens, and most of the houses have the shape of square lampshades; the palace resembles an Inca temple crossed with a bunker. Rataxes's name is carved on each side of the palace steps, with a letter left off from the beginning or the end each time, so that it deconstructs into words that include TAXES, AXES, and RAT.

Some readers have suggested that the country of the rhinos—which is more or less next door, and whose army wears black helmets and black boots that recall the costume of German soldiers in both World Wars—represents Eastern Europe, or even specifically Germany. Laurent de Brunhoff has denied this, but he agrees that the rhinos are essentially the opposite of the elephants, who are known for their peaceful nature, polite behavior, and love of beauty, flowers, recreation, and the arts. The rhinos, by contrast, are crude, impulsively aggressive, and prejudiced, lacking in both good taste and good manners.

We first hear of the rhinos in the second book of Jean de Brunhoff's original series, *The Travels of Babar*. While Babar and Celeste are on their honeymoon, their young cousin Arthur plays a trick on Rataxes, tying a firecracker to his tail. Though the wise old elephant Cornelius tries to make peace, Rataxes, who is "revengeful and mean," refuses his apologies and declares war. At first, the rhinos are victorious, and when Babar and Celeste return, they find the countryside devastated in a manner that recalls the battlefields of World War I: "A few broken trees! Is that all that is left of the great forest? There are no more flowers, no more birds. Babar and Celeste are very sad and weep as they see their ruined country."

Many elephants have been wounded, and are being treated in an outdoor field hospital by nurses in World War I costumes. Meanwhile, Rataxes is preparing another attack. Babar saves the day by a stratagem: he paints eyes on the rumps of his biggest soldiers, and colors their tails red, while Arthur makes red and green wigs for them out of leaves. Now, when they advance backwards, they look like monsters. The rhinos are terrified and retreat in disorder—essentially defeated by innovative fashion design.

The antagonism between the elephants and the rhinos increases in Laurent de Brunhoff's *Babar and the Wul-*

ly-Wully (1975). In this story, Babar's daughter Flora discovers a small, friendly, very rare creature with soft green fur. The Wully-Wully is so totally lovable and desirable that he is kidnapped by Rataxes and imprisoned in the city of the rhinos, from which he has to be rescued by Zephir. But almost as soon as the Wully-Wully returns to Celesteville, the rhino soldiers attack, "sweeping through Celesteville like a hurricane," and carrying off the Wully-Wully again. War is about to be declared, but Flora saves the day by going alone to see King Rataxes and persuading him that the Wully-Wully needs his freedom. Amazingly, the king agrees, and the last picture shows Flora and Rataxes together, rocking the Wully-Wully in a rope swing.

In 1978, in *Babar's Mystery*, one of the most exciting stories in the series, another disagreeable rhino appears. This time he is the leader of a criminal gang of low-life crocodiles; he wears a loud checked suit and smokes cigars. (The crocodiles are equally inelegant, in shabby tailcoats and sneakers.) He hangs out at the seaside resort of Celesteville-by-the Sea, which seems to be located in Brittany, near Mont-St-Michel, a picture of which appears in one double-page spread. The piano from the hotel is stolen, then Babar's red convertible, and finally the statue of an elephant from the town square. But in the end Arthur, with Babar's help, catches the thieves.

Out in the human world, as time passed, borders came down, and both France and Germany joined the European Union. Laurent de Brunhoff's attitude towards the country of the rhinos also seems to have changed. "I wanted to show that not all rhinos are bad," he recently told me. The result was *Babar's Little Girl Makes a Friend* (1990), in which Babar's youngest daughter Isabelle meets the agreeable Vic, the little son of King Rataxes. But not all rhinos are good, either, and when Rataxes discovers the friendship, he is furious. "We don't like elephants in Rhino City!" he shouts, and his wife is "terribly angry." "You cannot be friends with that little elephant," she tells her son. At the end of the story Rataxes is somewhat reconciled, but Lady Rataxes remains enraged and prejudiced. "Keep your daughter away from our son!" she says to Babar. But the next day the children are back together. The moral seems to be that though adult rhinos are often aggressive and prejudiced, there may be hope for the younger generation.

In Babar's world, women are not necessarily more tolerant and peace-loving. A couple of years later, in *Babar's Battle* (1992), Babar remarks that Rataxes hasn't bothered the elephants for a long time. He is contradicted by Celeste, who says "that could change in a second . . . Rataxes has caused trouble before, and he could again. I don't trust him." And in fact a "rhino witch" named Macidexia, who lives in a cave underneath the lake near Celesteville, and has terrible taste in clothes, has been urging Rataxes to destroy the elephants for some time. She inspires him to drain the lake, causing fish and plants to die. Babar discovers the plot and telephones Rataxes to complain, but Rataxes replies by declaring war. The elephants and the rhinos prepare for battle, both sides wearing medieval armor, whereupon Babar challenges Rataxes to single combat. He wins by blinding Rataxes with the reflections from his shield: metaphorically, reflected aggression destroys the aggressor. Peace and order are restored—though (at least according to the illustrations) no rhinos have been invited to the big swimming party at the end of the book.

Though Babar does not apparently age after the first three

books in the series, he does change. When he first becomes king, as Ann Hildebrand says, he is "a courteous, responsible adult, a benevolent, honest leader, and a faithful, caring husband and father." In the face of loss or danger he remains steady, rational, and capable. But in the sixties, seventies, and early eighties he does not always retain his calm self-confidence. *In Babar Loses His Crown* (1967) he also loses his cool: he becomes sad and disturbed and unable to eat dinner, and declares that he cannot go out in public. "What will it look like, this evening at the Opera?' he asks pathetically. "The king of the elephants, without his crown?" Later, in *Babar and the Ghost* (1981), he is baffled and confused by a mischievous spirit that only the very young can see. His children take advantage of the situation to become rude and play tricks on adults, and life in the capital city is disrupted by traffic jams and fender-benders caused by an apparently driverless car. It is not until the very end of the story that Babar manages to get the ghost to leave Celesteville.

A few years later, in *The Rescue of Babar* (1993), our hero undergoes what might be called a midlife crisis. Hidden within the crater of an extinct volcano not far from Celesteville, it turns out, is a beautiful city. Its steep hills and semi-classical architecture, Laurent de Brunhoff says, were inspired by Borabadur in Java. To me, however, the city closely resembles San Francisco. The elephants who live there have striped ears and wear togas. They are especially fond of the arts: Isabelle pays for a double ice-cream cone by singing "Happy Birthday."

Isabelle has come to this city alone to rescue her father Babar, who has been kidnapped by the striped elephants so that he can tell them stories. He is imprisoned on a high ledge, where he sleeps in a hammock like the one he was rocked in when he was a baby in the first picture of *The Story of Babar*. But when Isabelle tells him, "We have to get out of here, back to Celesteville," he does not want to go.

> "What for?" said Babar. "It's very pleasant here, and the striped elephants treat me with the greatest courtesy. Their music is enchanting, their food is delicious, and they only want me to tell them stories. Why should I leave?" "But you are King of the Elephants in Celesteville!" exclaimed Isabelle. "Let someone else be king," said Babar, and he fell back asleep.

At this point Babar has apparently regressed to childhood, abandoning his responsibilities as a ruler. It turns out later that in fact he has been drugged by doctored watermelon smoothies, and when their effect wears off he is willing to escape and return to Celesteville. But in the picture of Babar sneaking away from the city of the striped elephants at night, with Isabelle and her three animal companions, he is the only one who looks back—and while they appear happy and determined, his expression is one of doubt and regret.

Some readers who know that a few years before this book appeared, Laurent de Brunhoff moved from France to America, have seen *The Rescue of Babar* as a roman à clef. The striped elephants, in this view, are the Americans whose enthusiasm for the storyteller is so great that they want him here among them, in a country isolated from the rest of the world by its geography. However, since *The Rescue of Babar* our hero has clearly regained his poise and self-confidence.

Ann Hildebrand, in fact, connects this change to the end of Laurent de Brunhoff's first marriage, and his subsequent move to America and happy second marriage to the American writer and professor, Phyllis Rose. In fact, the text of *The Rescue of Babar*, like all the books that follow, is copyrighted in the name of Phyllis Rose, and for her the real point of the story is that it has a brave and active female protagonist.

Some fans of the Babar books have interpreted them as social, political, or personal fables; others have not hesitated to consider them as art and literature on the highest level. Nicholas Fox Weber, in *The Art of Babar* (1988), points out that both Jean and Laurent were art students and serious painters, and sees parallels between their work and that of classic European artists. There are comparisons to (in alphabetical order) Bonnard, Dufy, De Kooning, Delacroix, Giacometti, Klee, Matisse, Rubens, Jan van Eyck, and Pop Art. Laurent de Brunhoff says that in his view some of these comparisons "go too far." But it is also true that the landscape panoramas of Jean de Brunhoff's books sometimes recall the paintings of Dufy, and that the colors in many of Laurent de Brunhoff's illustrations—the intense reds and pinks and golden yellows, the flat greens—suggest Bonnard or Matisse.

Weber sees parallels between the original *Story of Babar* and the fiction of writers like Stendhal and Balzac. When Babar arrives in Paris as an adolescent, he is befriended by the very rich Old Lady. According to Weber, she is "a maternal figure, whose role is to provide the younger generation with worldly amenities." But she is also something more. In a way, her presence in the Babar books likens them to every French tale in which a young man from the country has a liaison with an older, more worldly woman. Babar is a kept man, the Old Lady his contented provider.

Nicholas Fox Weber also speculates on the differences between the Babar books of father and son. Although Laurent "has upheld the tradition of Babar through its characters and settings and maintained its essential personality," he feels that his is "a new, lighter, brighter universe," "highly charged, fluid, and animated," in which "painterly qualities have become more important than narrative ones." He remarks perceptively that in Jean de Brunhoff's world the danger level is high. This is true: Babar's mother is shot by a hunter, the previous king of the elephants dies by eating a poisonous mushroom, and soldiers are wounded in battle. In *Babar the King* (1933), the Old Lady is bitten by a snake and Cornelius is injured in a fire that destroys his house. That night Babar has his famous dream, in which Misfortune appears in the shape of "a frightful old woman surrounded by flabby ugly beasts"—Fear, Despair, Indolence, Sickness, Anger, Stupidity, Ignorance, Cowardice, Laziness, and Discouragement (a kind of long-nosed white pig). It takes twelve winged elephant angels to put them to flight. In Laurent's books, by contrast "the worst sort of occurrence consists of a character getting temporarily lost or slightly injured. . . . Above all, life is a series of joys."

Though the Babar books have been read and loved by children everywhere for over seventy years, they have also recently met with severe criticism. For example, they have been called anti-feminist. This attack, however, focuses on the early stories, written at a time when it was generally believed that women were essentially wives and mothers, whose careers should be limited to nursing, teaching, and the arts. Celeste dances in a circus, but only under duress, and once she has children, she stays home and takes care of them. The Old Lady serves as a nurse and a teacher, and at one point is said to be writing her memoirs. Later on, however, the female characters, particularly Isabelle, are much more active.

Herbert Kohl, the author of *Shall We Burn Babar?*, condemns the books, though reluctantly, as elitist. As a child he found them charming and wonderful; now, however, he thinks that they glorify capitalism and the ruling class:

> The Old Lady has money, lots of it. The source of her wealth is unclear. . . . It is clear that in the book the use of money and the earning of it are two totally different matters, and that it is perfectly normal and in fact delightful that some people have wealth they do not have to work for.

Kohl deplores Babar's "malleability and the good humor with which he jumps into becoming a well-dressed rich person-like elephant." He also complains that when Babar is chosen king because "he has learned so much living among men . . . all we are shown of his learning is that he knows how to choose clothes, order a meal at a restaurant, and add 2 + 2." Though his own early exposure to *The Story of Babar* apparently did not turn Kohl himself into an elitist, he believes that "[u]ncritical reading of the book is so potentially damaging that it should be withheld from children when possible."

The charge of colonialism is made most strongly by Ariel Dorfman. According to him, Babar is the primitive African who becomes a European and returns to "build a utopia with the willing aid of his native brothers." But his effort "is none other than the fulfillment of the dominant countries' colonial dream." In this dream, "the new ruler must come from the outside, a native instructed in the ways of men." The Babar books, Dorfman believes, teach the false moral that if backward countries imitate more advanced countries and import technological know-how, they will improve their lot. What is left out of the story is the "plundering, racism, undevelopment, and misery" that colonial policy often brings. This is of course true in a sense, but it is a charge that can be leveled at many utopian visions, and at almost all children's picture books, which normally portray a better world than the one we live in.

The accusation of racism in Babar rests largely on two books published before 1950. Today, the drawings of what the texts refer to as "cannibals" (*The Travels of Babar*) and "savages" (*Babar's Picnic*, 1949) seem shocking. When these books first appeared, however, much of both adult and children's culture was naïvely racist. White performers blacked their faces to resemble caricatures of African Americans, and a recurrent cartoon situation of the 1930s and '40s featured a pair of missionaries in a cook pot; *Doctor Doolittle* and *Little Black Sambo* were popular and much-admired children's books, and thousands of English and American children owned Golliwog or Mammy dolls.

Jean de Brunhoff had drawn caricatured Africans in *The Travels of Babar*, and they must have seemed a reasonable subject for his son Laurent, who was only twenty-three at the time *Babar's Picnic* was written. Soon, however, as people all over the world became aware of the hateful and harmful stereotyping of not only African but Asian and Native American people, Laurent was one of the first children's book artists to make amends and include realistic drawings of black people in his public scenes. In *Babar Comes to America* (1965) there are African Americans on the street in Chicago, New York, and Detroit: they are shown building automobiles, fishing from a pier along with whites, and at a Hollywood party. While in New York, Babar goes to hear "Theodorus Priest" (Thelonious Monk) and his jazz quartet, which includes two white and two black players.

For a long time Laurent de Brunhoff has regretted his early drawings of African "savages"; he decided years ago that *Babar's Picnic* will never be reprinted. Yet Random House, the original publisher of Jean de Brunhoff, continues to issue *The Travels of Babar*, with its stereotyped black "cannibals," and some adult readers still complain of its bias: the description of the book on the current Amazon site calls it "as far from politically correct as you can get."

Fortunately, I am especially lucky to have met Laurent de Brunhoff myself, in Key West, Florida, where he and his wife, the literary critic and biographer Phyllis Rose, have a house. He is as charming and original as his books, a dedicated gardener, and remarkably fit. Though he was over seventy when he and his wife first came to dinner at our house, he climbed our giant gumbo limbo tree with skill and speed even before drinks were served. Not surprisingly, he also turned out to be an expert yoga practitioner, and the author of a successful guidebook, *Yoga for Elephants*, in which Babar demonstrates the classic poses.

Saying No to Narnia

In 2005, an "epic fantasy film" titled *The Lion, the Witch and the Wardrobe* was released by Walt Disney Pictures in association with something called Walden Media. This organization, which is based in Los Angeles and appears to have no actual connection with Thoreau's pond or book, was founded by the Denver multibillionaire Philip Anschutz, an evangelical Christian and supporter of George W. Bush. The stated goal of Walden Media is to produce "family-friendly" movies—including films based on all seven of C. S. Lewis's *Chronicles of Narnia*. Their choice of this project is deeply appropriate, for the Narnia books have always been popular with conservative Christians, not only for their partly concealed religious message, but for their rather disturbing social and political implications.

The Disney/Walden version of *The Lion, the Witch, and the Wardrobe*, like the original book, is a fantasy in which four English children find their way into a world ruled by an evil

White Witch where it is always winter and never Christmas. With the help of some talking animals, especially a huge lion called Aslan, the Witch is eventually defeated, and spring returns to Narnia. The story can also be read as a Christian allegory in which the killing and resurrection of Aslan stands for the death and rebirth of Christ at Easter, complete with his expiation of the sins of mankind (in this case, a sulky ten-year-old called Edmund who has betrayed his brother and sisters to the White Witch out of sibling rivalry and a greedy passion for a candy called Turkish Delight).

The film is remarkably faithful to the original. Tilda Swinton, with a crown of ice and gray-blonde dreadlocks, is elegantly scary as the White Witch, and the computer-generated animals, including the traditionally domestic Beavers, who speak a kind of rural British dialect, are not too cute. The transition from the dark furry wardrobe to the bright snowy wood, which some psychologists have compared to a birth experience, is striking, and the landscape of Narnia is beautiful.

The scenes of Aslan's sacrificial death and resurrection, however, underline the religious allegory perhaps more heavily than Lewis would have liked. Aslan's progress towards the Stone Table is a juvenile version of Mel Brooks's *Passion of the Christ*, complete with ugly scorning and beating and spitting bystanders. Later, as Susan and Lucy watch by Aslan's body, their postures imitate those of the mourning women in religious paintings, and when Aslan reappears, the golden light behind him is High Baroque.

Disney publicists have shrewdly mounted two advertising campaigns for the film, one secular and one sacred. They did not want to scare any paying non-Christians away, but they knew that the Christian overtones of *The Lion, the Witch, and the Wardrobe* could make the film tremendously popular with the religious establishment, especially in America. *The Chronicles of Narnia* were already approved reading for church study groups: in the *National Review*, John J. Miller spoke of them as "the continuation of Sunday School by different means." According to some Christian websites, all seven volumes of the series can be profitably read as religious fables. *The Magician's Nephew* describes the creation of the world and the origin of evil, and contains a sacrament of marriage. *Prince Caspian* illustrates the corruption and restoration of true religion, and *The Horse and His Boy* tells the story of the conversion of a heathen. There is a spiritual voyage and a baptism in *The Voyage of the Dawn Treader*, and the *Descent into Hell* is featured in *The Silver Chair*. The final book of the series, *The Last Battle*, retells the coming of the Antichrist and the Last Judgment.

Even before the film opened, the Disney organization was targeting evangelical Protestantism, and a company called "Motive Entertainment" was sponsoring meetings for church officials and supporters in a hundred and forty American churches, encouraging the use of *The Chronicles of Narnia* as an inspirational text, with sample sermons available for download on the Web.

Conservative politicians also got into the act, though not without repercussions. When the governor of Florida, Jeb Bush, chose *The Lion, the Witch and the Wardrobe* for a statewide reading program, the *Palm Beach Post* called the move "a cabal of Christian commerce," and claimed that the state was "opening up the public schools to back door catechism lessons." An organization called Americans United for Sepa-

ration of Church and State then proposed to sue the State of
Florida over the issue.

C. S. Lewis, however, always claimed that *The Chronicles
of Narnia* was not allegorical. "You are mistaken when you
think that everything in the books 'represents' something in
the world," he wrote to a group of schoolchildren. "Things do
that in *The Pilgrim's Progress* but I'm not writing that way." It
is true that there is no consistent one-to-one parallel between
characters and events in Narnia and their religious equivalent, as there is in Bunyan's *Pilgrim's Progress*. But Lewis also
often spoke of the *Chronicles* as a means of awakening religious impulses in children who might be turned off by the
conventional teachings of Sunday school, as he had been.

Clive Staples Lewis, who was born in 1898 and grew up
in Northern Ireland, was raised as a low-church Anglican,
with an emphasis on religious observance as a duty. But by
the age of fourteen he had lost his faith in God—partly, perhaps, because his beloved mother had died of cancer when
he was nine in spite of his fervent prayers for her recovery.
His doubt and sense of abandonment were increased when
two weeks later he and his older brother Warren were sent
to an awful English boarding school that Lewis later called
"Belsen" in his autobiography. The headmaster of this school
had already been prosecuted for cruelty to his students when
Lewis arrived in 1908, and a few years later he would be cer-
tified insane.

Both boys wrote again and again to their father, begging
to come home, and Lewis prayed constantly for relief from
the constant savage beatings. But he did not escape "Belsen"
until it was closed in 1910. As a result, he not only became
estranged from God, but turned against his father, a pious,

temperamental lawyer of whom he later wrote, "His emotions had always been uncontrolled. Under the pressure of anxiety his temper became incalculable; he spoke wildly and acted unjustly." Lewis's next English school was only marginally better: he was awkward at games, and was constantly bullied and teased. "Holidays are Heaven, school is, well, death," he wrote.

According to his most recent biographer, Alan Jacobs, Lewis was rescued from adolescent depression and despair by the discovery of myth, romance, and fairy tale, and by intense Wordsworthian experience of the natural world— all of which he called 'Joy.' At fifteen he read Frazer's *The Golden Bough* and began to see Christianity as only another Near Eastern myth of a dying and reviving god. In December 1914 he was confirmed in a state of guilty disbelief.

For the next seventeen years, most of which Lewis spent at Oxford—first as a student and then as a tutor at Magdalen College, he regarded himself as an agnostic. It was not until September 1931, during a late-night discussion with two other Oxford scholars, Hugo Dyson and J. R. R. Tolkien, that he returned to Christianity. Lewis had been drawn to Tolkien, who was a practicing Catholic, because they both loved the myths and legends of Old English and Scandinavian folklore. That night, as they talked in Lewis's college rooms or strolled round Addison's Walk, Tolkien and Dyson persuaded Lewis that the Christian myth was not only equally beautiful and powerful, but also true. Lewis's conversion was completed nine days later on a trip to the zoo, where he "made friends with a bear whom he nicknamed Bultitude." As he reported later, "When we set out I did not believe that Jesus Christ is the Son of God, and when we reached the zoo I did."

Though Lewis had a great deal to say about his spiritual history, he was secretive about his private life, a circumstance that has made things difficult for his biographers. The central mystery is his thirty-two-year relationship with Mrs. Janie Moore, the mother of an army friend. Before they went overseas in 1917, Lewis and Patrick Moore agreed that if one of them was killed, the other would look after their single parent. (Lewis's father was a widower; Mrs. Moore was estranged from her husband, though never divorced.) Patrick did die in France; his mother moved to Oxford, and for over thirty years Lewis kept his word—and perhaps more than his word. Though he slept in his college rooms during the week, he spent most of his time at Mrs. Moore's house, and went on extended holidays with her and her daughter, Maureen. Lewis always refused to discuss the relationship with his friends, and concealed it as much as possible from everyone else.

Today Janie Moore remains an ambiguous figure. Some of Lewis's friends spoke of her as self-centered and completely unintellectual; others reported her as charming. Both A. N. Wilson and Alan Jacobs believe that the relationship was sexual, and Wilson suggests that it had something of a sado-masochistic element. Mrs. Moore spoke of Lewis as being "as good as an extra maid," and many observers were amazed at the way he waited on her. He also largely supported her and her daughter financially for many years.

When they met, Janie Moore was "a pretty blonde Irish-woman" of forty-five and Lewis was eighteen; by the time he became a practicing Christian, she was fifty-nine and he was thirty-two. (It is possible that Lewis's conversion to Christianity, with its commandment against adultery, ended an erotic connection that might by then have been a burden.)

As she grew older and her health failed, Mrs. Moore became difficult and demanding. Lewis remained devoted; even after she had more or less lost her mind, he visited her in the nursing home every day. Lewis's brother Warren, a retired soldier who had shared Mrs. Moore's house (which he helped to buy) for twenty years, spoke of her death in 1951 as the end of a "mysterious self imposed slavery."

The other romantic relationship in Lewis's life is far better documented—perhaps over-documented. Lewis's friendship with and marriage to his American fan Joy Davidman, and her subsequent death from cancer, has been the subject of many articles and books, a play, a film, and several television dramas. Most of them portray the relationship as a tragic but uplifting romance. For Lewis, Joy Davidman's appearance in his life must have seemed extraordinary. Though he was a famous writer, he was also a heavy fifty-four-year-old man with a booming voice, shabbily dressed and awkward around women. ("I am tall, fat, bald, red-faced, double-chinned . . . and wear glasses. . . ." he had recently written to a class of fifth-graders in America who asked for a description of himself.) Joy was thirty-seven. She was small, dark, attractive, lively, tough, and outspoken, a nonpracticing Jew and former Communist from New York.

Joy regarded C. S. Lewis as one of the greatest men of his time, whose works had inspired her conversion to Christianity. She began writing him fan mail in 1950, and in 1952 came to England in order to meet him. (The coincidence of her first name with Lewis's private term for peak experiences of literature and nature appeared miraculous to both of them; certainly it was the hidden message in the title he later chose for his autobiography, *Surprised by Joy*.)

Joy Davidman was certainly a surprise to Lewis's friends. Their opinions of her varied widely: some saw her as a vulgar and scheming husband-hunter, others as an intelligent, amusing woman who had rescued him from loneliness and despair after Mrs. Moore's death. When presently Joy moved to Oxford, Lewis began seeing her every day; soon he was paying her rent and the school fees of her two sons. Though he continued to declare himself a "confirmed bachelor," in 1956, in order to prevent Joy from being deported from England, they were joined in a civil ceremony. But Lewis did not consider himself truly married in the Christian sense; he told one friend that it was "a pure matter of friendship and expediency . . . simply a legal form." It was not until the following year, when Joy was apparently dying of cancer, that they were married by an Anglican priest in her hospital room.

The priest who performed the marriage ceremony also prayed for Joy's healing, and whether the cause was spiritual or psychological, the effect was remarkable. Joy's cancer went into remission; and for the next three and a half years she and Lewis enjoyed a full life together. As Lewis put it, rather embarrassingly, they "feasted on love." Joy went everywhere with him, and he even tried to include her in the regular Thursday meetings of his all-male discussion group, the Inklings. A. N. Wilson reports that those friends "who were forced to meet Joy did not enjoy it, and pretty soon made excuses to avoid meeting her again." Lewis also took her to Greece, which she had always longed to visit, and consulted her about his writing. But then Joy's cancer returned, and she died in July 1959.

Biographers and critics have tried to understand how Lewis could have chosen to devote his life to two such different but equally demanding women. One possible explanation comes from Lewis's father, Albert, who wrote to Lewis's brother that his younger son was "an impetuous, kind-hearted creature who could be cajoled by any woman who has been through the mill." It is also true that both Janie Moore and Joy Davidman were evidently very much in love with Lewis and regarded him as a truly great man—something that is often irresistible. And both seem to have had an effect on his writing: the domestic heroine of Lewis's science-fiction fantasy, *That Hideous Strength*, is named Jane, and the more active and adventurous girls in the later *Chronicles of Narnia*, like Shasta in *The Horse and His Boy* and Polly in *The Magician's Nephew*, surely owe something to Joy Davidman.

Many critics who first read *The Chronicles of Narnia* as children report being unaware of its Christian meanings or of any other hidden messages, but several have complained that when they reread the books as adults, they were shocked and dismayed. In *Revisiting Narnia*, a diverse collection of present and former fans (it includes a Catholic, a liberal feminist, an agnostic, a New Age witch, a postmodernist, and several popular authors of fantasy) both praise and criticize Lewis. Other readers have been wholly negative. One is the immensely gifted and popular British writer Philip Pullman, author of the best-selling trilogy, *His Dark Materials*, who has described himself as a Christian atheist. Pullman has denounced the Narnia books as religious propaganda, and called the series "ugly and poisonous." He has summed up their message as "Death is better than life, boys are better than girls; light-colored people are better than dark-colored people, and so on."

Some generally favorable critics, too, have expressed doubts about the portrayal of Jesus as the huge, beautiful,

and terrible lion Aslan. In most juvenile classics, they point
out, the heroes and heroines tend to be relatively small and
powerless; they are mice, rabbits, dogs, cats, hobbits, and of
course, children. They win through moral rather than physical strength, because they possess the standard folk-tale qualities of intelligence, courage, kindness, and luck. But Lewis
believed in what used to be called "muscular Christianity,"
which preferred to represent Jesus as athletic, masculine,
and even militant. This may have been responsible for the
selection of a lion the size of a small elephant as the Narnian
representation of Jesus, rather than the traditional innocent,
meek and mild Lamb of God. A better choice, Adam Gopnik
suggested in *The New Yorker*, would have been "a lowly and
bedraggled donkey" who is killed by lions but finally reappears "as the king of all creation."

Aslan does appear to Lucy and Eustace in the form of a
lamb at the end of *The Voyage of the Dawn Treader*, when they
are about to return to their own world; and as a cat in *The
Horse and His Boy*, but he soon reassumes his original shape
and power. Even before they meet him, the mere sound of
his name, which means "lion" in Turkish, causes joy in good
characters and horror in those who are under an evil spell.
(One probable source for the figure of Aslan is the fantasy
novel, *The Place of the Lion* [1931] by Lewis's friend Charles
Williams. In this book, the Platonic archetypes appear in
three-dimensional form: a huge lion represents strength and
kingship. Aslan may also be a version of the Biblical Lion of
Judah). When Lucy cries that she cannot bear to live in her
world without Aslan, he says that he is there, too. "But there
I have another name. This was the very reason why you were
brought to Narnia, that by knowing me here for a little, you

may know me better there." Several critics have seen this as an obvious reference to Jesus Christ, but it is possible that for readers of other faiths it might have other associations.

Lewis, like many fundamentalist Christians, emphasizes Jesus over God the Father; indeed in some ways he goes even further than they usually do. In *The Chronicles of Narnia* Aslan declares that he is the "Son of the Emperor over Sea," but this figure never appears. It is Aslan, not the Emperor, who creates the world by singing it into being; and it is he who oversees the apocalypse that ends *The Last Battle*.

The religious controversy is not the only one swirling around Narnia. Lewis has also been charged with racism as a result of his portrait of the Calormenes in *The Horse and His Boy* and *The Last Battle*. Calormene (apparently from the Latin word for heat, calor) is a desert country far to the south of Narnia. Its people are dark-skinned and prone to violence; the men wear turbans and carry scimitars, and their diet is heavy on oil, rice, and garlic. They are cruel to animals and worship a four-armed god with a vulture's head who loves blood and demands human sacrifice. The rulers of Calormene are autocratic, corrupt, treacherous, and brutal; slavery is common, and most women cannot read or write or chose their husbands. However successful the film of *The Lion, the Witch and the Wardrobe* may be, it is hard to see how *The Horse and His Boy* could be made into a sequel without serious political and cultural repercussions.

Other critics have seen Lewis's books for children as anti-feminist. In Narnia, as Philip Pullman points out, girls almost always come second to boys. They have fewer adventures, and none has a book named after her. In the early stories girls usually stay well out of the fighting, or at a safe distance.

Though Susan is a skilled archer, she does not take part in the battle at the end of *The Lion, the Witch and the Wardrobe*, and Lucy appears only after everything is over, to cure wounds with the magic potion Father Christmas has given her.

In Narnia there is also no such thing as a good, strong supernatural female figure. The embodiment of virtuous power is always male, while the embodiment of evil power is the White Witch, who appears to be based partly on Hans Christian Andersen's evil Snow Queen and partly on George MacDonald's North Wind (who is really Death, and rules over a kingdom of ice and snow); both of them also abduct and enchant a little boy.

The Narnia books also diverge from the pattern set by one of C. S. Lewis's favorite juvenile authors, E. Nesbit, from whom he also borrowed a good deal. In Nesbit's *The Five Children* the protagonists are four temporarily parentless siblings, two of each gender (the fifth child is a year-old baby who only complicates the action). Like Lewis's characters, they travel in time and space and meet fabulous creatures. The book some consider Nesbit's masterpiece, *The Enchanted Castle*, also features two boys and two girls, and has a plot in which figures from prehistory and Greek mythology appear. But where Lewis was an old-fashioned Tory, Nesbit was a Fabian socialist and a feminist. Her children have little interest in religion: the clergymen in her books are kind but clueless, and the temporal and spiritual authorities the children meet on their travels are often cruel and dishonest. Nesbit's characters do not get much help from adults; instead they learn to rely on their own intelligence and courage, and it is often the girls rather than the boys who confront dangers and solve problems.

Some contemporary criticism of C. S. Lewis, though

justified, may be partly excused on the grounds that he was subject to the beliefs and prejudices of his time and place. His dislike and suspicion of Oriental countries, and his preference for all things Northern and for heroes who are fair and fair-haired, were typical of conservative writers of his generation. As a conventionally educated man born in 1898 and living most of his life in the then almost completely masculine environment of Oxford, he might have assumed that girls were weaker, less interesting, and more fearful than boys. This might also explain his distaste for whatever at the time was seen as typically feminine—and, to judge by what happens at the end of the series, his apparent dislike of most adult women.

Many readers have been infuriated by Lewis's final condemnation of Susan Pevensie, the former wise and gentle Queen Susan, as "no longer a friend of Narnia," in *The Last Battle*. She is cast out of Paradise forever because at twenty-one she speaks of her earlier experiences as only a childhood fantasy, and is "too keen on being grown up" and "interested in nothing nowadays except nylons and lipstick and invitations." Apart from the fact that these seem very minor sins, it is hard to believe that Susan could have changed that much and forgotten her happiness in Narnia and her commitment to Aslan. Apologists have claimed that her banishment was necessary to demonstrate that even those who have once been saved can fall from grace. Nevertheless it seems deeply unfair to many readers that Edmund, Susan's younger brother, who has betrayed the others to the White Witch, is allowed to repent and become King Edmund, while Susan, whose faults are much less serious, is not given the opportunity.

It has been suggested that some of the problems in the

Narnia books arose because Lewis himself did not take them as seriously as his works for adults like *The Allegory of Love* and *Mere Christianity*. Readers have also been made uneasy by his anachronistic and indiscriminate borrowings from other sources. In *The Lion, the Witch and the Wardrobe*, for instance, there are not only giants and dwarfs and a witch from Northern European folktales, but a whole zoo of talking animals, including two badgers who seem to have waddled straight out of Beatrix Potter. There is also a large population of fauns, satyrs, dryads, nymphs, and centaurs from Greek mythology, plus a character who only appeared in the popular imagination in the nineteenth century: Father Christmas with his sleigh pulled by reindeer.

J. R. R. Tolkien, who was a close friend of Lewis's, spent decades planning the world of *The Lord of the Rings*, giving it a consistent geography, an elaborate history, and several languages. He hated *The Lion, the Witch and the Wardrobe*, regarding it as too rapidly and carelessly put together out of mismatched scraps. Yet Tolkien has been overruled by generations of readers who forgive Lewis's faults because of his occasional moments of imaginative triumph, some of which involve incongruous juxtapositions. The scene at the beginning of *The Lion, the Witch and the Wardrobe*, when Lucy goes through a clothes-cupboard and comes out into a snowy winter landscape lit by a London street lamp and meets a faun carrying an umbrella and several brown-paper parcels, proves that sometimes anachronism can be magical.

Tolkien's invented world has been described as Anglo-Saxon or pre-medieval. One perceptive critic, Mary Frances Zambreno, an American medievalist, suggests that Lewis based Narnia on the concepts of time and space and history that prevailed in the Middle Ages. In Narnia, she points out, just as in the Middle Ages, history is seen as finite. The world was created at a specific time and will be destroyed at another specific time. (According to the Lewis expert Walter Hooper, Narnia lasts exactly 2,555 years.) Outside of heaven, there is no idea of infinity or of progress. Like Earth in medieval maps, Narnia is the center of its universe. Aslan's homes are far to the east or west; Calormen, to the south, "corresponds to the Islamic Kingdoms of the Middle Ages, complete with deserts, Moors, and exotic walled cities" as well as pagan gods. Paradise is a walled garden with a fountain in the center. "'Narnia' was also a word known to medieval scholars— it was the name given by the Romans to the ancient Umbrian city Nequinium."

Another possible interpretation of the stories occurred to me while I was watching the film of *The Lion the Witch, and the Wardrobe*, in which the computer-generated Aslan is halfway between a animation Lion King and an animal you might see in the zoo or a circus. What he most resembles, however, is the traditional British Lion, that ubiquitous nineteenth-century symbol of Empire, visible in hundreds of cartoons and frozen in stone in front of hundreds of public buildings. Possibly *The Chronicles of Narnia* could be seen not only as a fairy tale or a religious allegory, but also as a history of the creation, prosperity, and eventual destruction of the British Empire. In its prime, Narnia, like Britain, controlled the sea and set up outposts on distant islands. But by the time of *The Last Battle* the country has been weakened and invaded by ugly aliens and godless foreigners. Most of its territory has been lost, and the land is ecologically devastated. Antichrist has appeared in the form of an ape named

Shift. In the end the country is totally destroyed. Aslan, his human allies, and the talking animals and minor gods escape into a kind of super-Narnian heaven ("higher up and further in") only by dying as an empire—and becoming history and literature.

Perhaps the most important, though least obvious, way in which the Narnia books differ from most classics of juvenile literature is that they do not free children from the authority of adults. In most of the classic stories heroes and heroines have adventures and face dangers on their own; they solve problems and defeat their adversaries with only occasional help and advice from grown-ups. Often the good adults turn out to be unable to help the heroes and heroines very much, as in the *Harry Potter* books. And even when they seem to be on your side, adults may turn out to be weak or corrupt; at times it seems best not to trust anyone over fifteen. In some recent children's fiction, such as Lemony Snicket's popular *Series of Unfortunate Events*, the grown-ups are usually stupid, selfish, actively evil, or all of these things at once. The implicit lesson of such tales is subversive; they suggest that though some adults may wish you well, and may give you the knowledge or skills that will help you through life, essentially you are going to be on your own.

In the Narnia books, by contrast, children only seem to be on their own. Behind everything that happens is the power and wisdom and intention of Aslan. Usually disaster can only be avoided by Aslan's visible or invisible intervention. With his aid battles are won, souls saved, and enemies defeated. Even when he does not seem to be there, he is: in *The Horse and His Boy* Shasta learns that Aslan has already preserved his life four times when he thought that chance, luck, or his own skill had done so. Without Aslan's help, all seven books tell us, we would fail and evil would conquer. As Alan Jacobs writes, this is "a narrative world in which obedience to just Authority brings happiness and security, while neglect of that same Authority brings danger and misery." Or, as Russell W. Dalton puts it in *Revisiting Narnia*, "The ultimate virtue in Narnia, it seems, is to submit completely to the will of Aslan." The attitude of the good characters in the Narnia books towards Aslan is one of almost abject love and adoration mixed with literally holy terror. "That is the greatest joy in life, even if it leads to trials and . . . death." Other characters in the stories "are called upon to be good and faithful, but they should not presume that they can really accomplish any good."

It is no surprise that conservative Christians admire these books. They teach us to accept authority; to love and follow our leaders instinctively, as the children in the Narnia books love and follow Aslan. By implication, they suggest that we should and will admire and fear and obey whatever impressive-looking and powerful authority figures we come in contact with. They also suggest that without the help of Aslan (that is, of such powerful figures, or their representatives on earth) we are bound to fail. Alone, we are weak and ignorant and helpless. Individual initiative is limited; almost everything has already been planned out for us in advance, and we cannot know anything or achieve anything without the help of God.

This is, of course, the kind of mind-set that evangelical churches prefer and cultivate; the kind that makes people vote against their own economic and social interests, that makes successful, attractive, and apparently intelligent young

men and women want to become the apprentices of Donald
Trump, or of much worse rich and powerful figures. This
mind-set could even be called deluded, since in this world, as
we know, a giant lion does not usually appear to see that the
right side wins and all the good people are happy. In Narnia,
faith in Aslan, who comes among his followers and speaks
to them, may make sense: but here on earth, as the classic
folktales have told us for generations, it is better to depend on
your own courage and wit and skill, and the good advice of
less than omnipotent beings.

Harry Potter Revisited

In international folklore, one of the best-known tales is of a poor, hungry child who wishes that the family's pot of porridge were always full. The wish is granted—and often more than granted. No matter how much is scooped from the pot, porridge continues to boil up, slopping over the stove, then onto the floor, filling the cottage, surging out the door, and eventually almost drowning the whole village.

With this tale in mind, imagine a dark, wet winter day in Edinburgh. A young single mother, living on welfare, is sitting in a café because there is no heat in her rented apartment. Whenever her baby falls asleep for a while in its stroller, she tries to write a children's story that she first thought of more than two years ago. Suddenly a fairy appears and offers her three wishes. She asks modestly that she may be able to finish her book, that it may be published, and that children all over the world may read it.

As with the irrepressible pot of porridge, J. K. Rowling gets more than her wish. The story is finished, the publisher found, and the tales of Harry Potter begin to cover the earth, both as books (they have now been translated into over sixty languages) and as films. There are games, toys, costumes, guidebooks, websites, and a multitude of imitative versions of the novels that bear the same relation to the originals as wet cardboard sludge does to tasty porridge. In China alone, according to the *New York Times*, there are already a dozen false Harry Potter books in print, in one of which six Chinese teenage wizards travel to Hogwarts to rescue Harry and his friends from the forces of evil.

The film versions of Rowling's books are, fortunately, very good. By now it sometimes seems as if every great British stage and screen actor has appeared in them. The casts have included Helena Bonham Carter, John Cleese, Ralph Fiennes, Michael Gambon, Robert Hardy, Richard Harris, Maggie Smith, Miranda Richardson, Alan Rickman, Fiona Shaw, Emma Thompson, and Zoe Wanamaker. In the film *The Order of the Phoenix*, Imelda Staunton, best known to Americans as the kind and sympathetic heroine of *Vera Drake*, is the villainess. She appears as Dolores Umbridge, a brilliantly chosen name that suggests a down-to-earth mum from *Coronation Street*.

At first this association seems reasonable: Professor Umbridge, who has been appointed to teach Defense Against the Dark Arts at Hogwarts, is plump, middle-aged, and always smiling; she wears pink tweed, with perky bows in her curly permed hair, and speaks in sweet, ingratiating tones. Soon, though, the picture darkens. Professor Umbridge refuses to allow her students to practice her subject, confining their class time to the reading and rereading of theory (a frustration that many recent graduate students in the humanities have also suffered). Eventually she turns out to be ambitious and relentlessly cruel. When we take another look at her name, we are likely to think that we should have known this from the start, since "Dolores Umbridge" so clearly suggests grief (dolor) and resentment (umbrage). Names in Rowling's books, like those in Dickens, are always significant: "Harry," for instance, recalls both Shakespeare's brave and impulsive Prince Hal and his Harry Hotspur, while "Voldemort" simultaneously suggests theft, mold, and death.

The delight that all these great actors appear to feel in taking a holiday from serious drama and hamming it up, sometimes against type, is often practically visible on the screen. As the formidable but benevolent witch Professor McGonagall, for instance, Dame Maggie Smith cannot help reminding us of a reformed Miss Jean Brodie, now genuinely concerned for her students' welfare and no longer a fan of Mussolini, but bitterly opposed to the authoritarianism of the Ministry of Magic. Sir Michael Gambon, as the headmaster of Hogwarts, Professor Dumbledore, recalls the TV show based on the novels of Georges Simenon, where as Inspector Maigret he also often arrived late but triumphantly at the solution to a dramatic problem. It is easy to imagine them and their colleagues getting together for laughter and congratulations at the end of every scene.

Meanwhile, J. K. Rowling has become the richest and most famous children's writer in the world. Already in 1999 more than two thousand fans lined up outside a bookshop to meet her and have their copies of *The Prisoner of Azkaban* signed. At this occasion, according to *Publishers Weekly*, "the crowd became so ugly that the store manager was bitten and punched." Soon Rowling could not leave the house without being pointed out and besieged by fans. By 2001, in an interview on the BBC, she complained that people had started searching her trash. "It's horrible," she said. "It feels like such an invasion, and I'm not a politician, I'm not an entertainer; I never expected that level of interest in my life."

That Rowling has in fact received far more attention than she ever wanted is strongly substantiated by the attitude of her hero to his own fame. Again and again he expresses the wish that he were an ordinary boy. In *Harry Potter and the Order of the Phoenix*, for instance, he says, "He was sick of it, sick of being the person who was stared at and talked about all the time." But Harry is not only oppressed by public attention: he is also, as the books progress, in more and more danger of being injured or killed. In the real world, too, this is an occupational hazard of great fame and fortune, and one that Rowling now cannot help but share. She has already been stalked by a mentally disturbed fan, as well as sued (unsuccessfully) for plagiarism, and has received special permission from the Edinburgh City Council to increase the height of the walls surrounding her house and install an electronic security system.

Many writers, including myself, have speculated about why (ruling out supernatural influence) the Harry Potter books should have become so popular. The simplest explanation, perhaps, is that Rowling's stories have something for everyone, and combine so many popular genres: fantasy, school story, quest tale, thriller, mystery, and—more recently—electronic games. Some chapters of each book read like text versions of an early video game, in which cartoon characters whoosh about on screen trying to zap one another. Rowling also provides a wide selection of characters for readers to identify with. The student population of Hogwarts, like that of most high schools, is divided into jocks, brains, nice guys, and dangerous Goths. Harry and his two best friends are in the jock house, Griffindor, where "dwell the brave at heart." Ravenclaw emphasizes "wit and learning," while the students in Hufflepuff are described as "just and loyal." (In fact, Hermione seems a natural Ravenclaw and Ron a Hufflepuff; authorial convenience rather than the Sorting Hat appears to have placed them all together.) Unlike most classic boarding-school story locations, Hogwarts is multicultural and multiclass: its students come from both rich and poor families and include Chinese, Indian, Black, and Jewish kids. Some have parents who are also wizards or witches; others do not.

It has always been clear that J. K. Rowling writes extremely well and has remarkable powers of invention. She has created a world that cannot help but appeal to children and adolescents: one in which conventional adults (Muggles) are either clueless or cruel or both, while her young hero and his friends have special abilities. These abilities can also be seen as a metaphor for the particular powers of childhood and youth: imagination, energy, creativity, and especially humor—as well as being exciting, the books are often very funny.

In a world that is changing too rapidly even for many children to keep up with, the Harry Potter books can also be enjoyed as the celebration of a largely pre-industrial society. Hogwarts School is in a castle lit by torches and oil lamps and heated by fires; mail is carried by owls, and at the Ministry of Magic memos fly about as paper airplanes. There are no computers, phones, or radios, though a Knight Bus makes an occasional and often disastrous appearance. Magic takes the place of most modern inventions, and many of the people who employ it are children and adolescents. (Anyone who has recently had to appeal to a nine-year-old to debug a computer, program a cell phone, or operate the new TV's remote control will already have experienced the bafflement and irritation that Harry's Muggle foster parents, the Dursleys, frequently feel towards his unique skills.)

In interviews, J. K. Rowling has often said that as time passes her books would get darker, and she has been true to her word. When the final volume, *Harry Potter and the Deathly Hallows*, begins, Lord Voldemort and his associates, the Death Eaters, have taken over the three central institutions of the wizarding world: the Ministry of Magic, Hogwarts, and *The Daily Prophet* newspaper. Voldemort's political platform is racist and reactionary: it favors the limitation of magic power to "purebloods," all of whose ancestors were wizards and witches, and the elimination of what he and his friends scornfully call "Mudbloods" (those who have magical powers although both of their parents were Muggles) and "half-bloods," who had only one magically gifted parent. *The Daily Prophet* and its unscrupulous columnist Rita Skeeter are doing their best to promote these racist views, and to destroy the posthumous reputation of Professor Dumbledore, claiming that "he took an unnatural interest" in Harry Potter, and even suggesting that Harry may have been responsible for Dumbledore's death.

Lord Voldemort, who himself is a half-blood, is essentially interested not in racial purity but in total power and immortality. Since it has been prophesied that either he or Harry Potter must die, one of his first priorities is to kill our hero. He has already tried to protect his own life in a manner familiar to folklorists, by hiding his soul, or life force, in various external objects. As long as these objects, known here as Horcruxes, survive, he is safe. Much of the action of *Harry Potter and the Deathly Hallows* consists of the attempts of Harry and his friends to escape Voldemort and his followers, and at the same time to find and destroy the Horcruxes. Unable to return to Hogwarts, they spend most of the fall term on the run, living in a magical self-erecting tent that moves constantly around Britain in order to escape pursuit. They are often wet and cold and hungry and sometimes given to squabbling and sulking. At times, this part of the story resembles the worst camping-out experience you have ever had; at others, it recalls a dungeons-and-dragons-type electronic game. At one point, for instance, Harry and his friends escape from the underground vault of a bank run by goblins by clinging to the back of an old blind dragon whom they have liberated. The dragon is unaware of their presence, and never recognizes them as its rescuers—something that also occasionally happens to benefactors in Muggle life.

Though Harry Potter would prefer to be an ordinary person, he is clearly not one: even his role in the school game of Quidditch proves this. During matches he does not engage with the members of either team. Instead, as Seeker, he pursues a flying golden ball called the Snitch, which if captured will win points for his side. As the story progresses, it becomes apparent that Harry is not just a unique protagonist, but also an example of a mythical figure that the famous scholar Lord Raglan called the Hero. Though he is still only seventeen at the end of the story, he already scores six points on Raglan's list of the characteristics of the Hero:

1. At birth or soon after an attempt is made to kill him, but
2. he is spirited away, and
3. is reared by foster parents in a far country [among Muggles in Surrey, not all that far geographically from the Wizarding world, but supernaturally totally separated from it] . . .
4. On reaching manhood he returns or perhaps goes to his future kingdom [Hogwarts]"
5. He achieves "a victory over . . . a dragon or wild beast," as well as a series of evil opponents, both human and non-human.
6. Finally, he meets up with a mysterious death.

But there are other mythic echoes in this story. At one point in the saga, for instance, Lord Voldemort tries to convince Harry to join him by promising him power and immortality, the standard temptations of Satan. And at the end of *The Deathly Hallows*, having learned that one of Voldemort's external souls resides in his own body, Harry willingly goes into the forest to be killed by the Dark Lord, a self-sacrificial act that cannot help but recall the West's most familiar myth. After he dies, he returns to consciousness in a huge hall full of white mist that resembles King's Cross Station (where Muggle trains leave for Scotland, Rowling's home, and also where the train to Hogwarts departs from Track 9 3/4). This location for the afterlife cannot help but focus attention on the name of the London railway terminus, and suggest that we are in the realm of Christian tradition; another, earlier clue is that Lord Voldemort, the representation of evil, looks like a snake and is often accompanied by one.

In the transfigured King's Cross Station, Harry meets the spirit of Professor Dumbledore. He is offered the opportunity to "go on" or to return to Hogwarts and confront Lord Voldemort for the final time—in other words, to be resurrected.

Naturally, being a hero, Harry makes the second choice. His apparently dead body is carried back to the castle and displayed to his grieving friends, while the representatives of evil mock him and them. Then Harry springs to life, duels wand to wand with Voldemort, and defeats him. Virtue triumphs, and both Hogwarts and the Ministry of Magic—as well as, one hopes, *The Daily Prophet*— are returned to the control of relatively benevolent leaders.

Among readers, opinion about this ending varies. Some people I have talked to, including teenagers, are happy that Harry survives; others had not only expected that he would die in the end, but would have preferred it that way. Indeed, Rowling's repeated assurances to journalists that "there would be deaths" suggested this. (Over fifty people do die in *The Deathly Hallows*, but most of them are anonymous or minor characters; the most prominent and most missed by my informants are Fred Weasley and Dobby the house-elf.)

Almost everyone I've spoken to hated and regretted the Epilogue to *The Deathly Hallows*, which takes place nineteen years later in King's Cross Station and portrays Harry Potter and Ginny Weasley as parents of three children, two of whom are about to take the train for Hogwarts. Though many of the other passengers appear to stare at Harry, it seems clear that Rowling has at last given her hero the ordinary domestic life he longed for (and the same number of children she has). Also present are Hermione and Ron, now married and with two children, one of whom is also boarding the train. We are given no news of any of the other characters in the series except for Neville Longbottom, who is currently Hogwarts' Professor of Herbology. The fact that Harry's scar has not hurt in nineteen years does not mean that evil has vanished from the world.

Hogwarts still has a Slytherin House, whose students "use any means / To achieve their ends." Apparently, one out of four potential wizards is still drawn to the dark side. The Epilogue also effectively blocks the creation of more Harry Potter stories, since there can be no real suspense in any adventures he might have had in the past nineteen years—or even in the future. "Anyhow," as one fourteen-year-old reader from Santa Cruz put it, "who would care once they know he's just an ordinary middle-aged dad?"

The bitter criticism of *Harry Potter* that greeted its early success, mostly from fundamentalist Christians who objected to any story with a good witch or wizard in it (including *The Wizard of Oz*) seems to have died down somewhat. Complaints that Harry, Ron, and Hermione are not model children: that they break rules, disobey orders, and sometimes even lie or steal, are also less frequent—though of course these charges are true. Possibly, as the heroes of the book become older, such actions seem more readily justified, especially as Hogwarts begins to be infiltrated by teachers who are determined to injure or kill Harry and his friends.

Today criticism tends to be more analytical, in both senses of the word. In *The Psychology of Harry Potter* (2007), many of the contributing authors (like its editor), have PhDs in psychology, and occasionally a fairly tongue-in-cheek attitude towards their subject. They complain, however, that Hogwarts seems to feature rote learning, does not teach critical thinking, and lacks adequate career counseling. They also identify Harry's and Ron's relationship problems as due to their upbringing. Ron, one of seven children in a poor family, suffers from Anxiety Syndrome as the result of a lack of sustained parental attention and affection; Harry, raised in isolation by unloving relatives, suffers from Avoidance Syndrome. (Hermione, by contrast, had loving and attentive parents, and is an example of security and confidence.) Timely intervention by a well-trained Muggle child psychologist might have made their lives easier, but probably not much could have been done for Tom Riddle, the future Lord Voldemort, who was rejected at birth by his mother and brought up in a harsh orphanage, where he developed a full-blown antisocial personality disorder.

Looking back on the series now, some questions occur. For one thing, it is hard to understand why so many witches and wizards would want to join the Dark Lord and become Death Eaters. Voldemort is neither beautiful nor charming, as many Dark Lords have been in the past, both in history and in literature. His aspect is repellent and his manner towards his associates cold, haughty, and cruel. On the other hand, many of the Death Eaters themselves are fascinating in their own way, and so are their supernatural helpers. One of Rowling's best inventions is the Dementors, who wear black hooded cloaks, have scabby claw-like hands, and spread hopelessness and depression wherever they go. When they appear, they awaken your worst memories, and nothing seems good or beautiful or interesting or worth doing. The Dementors are the manifestation of emotions we are all subject to at times; and they also recall some people we have had the misfortune to know, people who have the ability to make life seem worse just by walking into the room and making a few apparently harmless remarks. (Examples from my own experience: "Of course, at your age a broken leg never heals completely, you'll probably always walk with a limp." "What a shame that your article should have appeared in a magazine that nobody ever reads.")

One way of looking at the Harry Potter books today, of course, is as a political allegory. At the start of the series, the Ministry of Magic, which seems to be located in Downing Street, is merely a bureaucracy handicapped by too many rules and a few pompously fussy officials. Later it appears to be run by fools whose main wish is to avoid trouble, and who therefore refuse to admit that Lord Voldemort has returned and that the entire Wizarding world is in danger. Gradually it becomes clear that some government officials can be bribed and manipulated. In *The Order of the Phoenix*, the Minister of Magic, Fudge (note his name), is seen talking to the rich and powerful Lucius Malfoy by Mr. Weasley, Ron's father. Mr .Weasley, who is basically a good man, but rather weak and ineffective, remarks, "Malfoy's been giving generously to all sorts of things for years. . . . Gets him in with the right people. . . . then he can ask favors . . . delay laws he doesn't want passed."

Another possible political parallel concerns the Prison of Azekaban. This is an isolated place far to the east where those judged to be evildoers are exiled by the Ministry and tortured by Dementors. When the series began, it was unlikely that many readers would associate Azekaban with actual and notorious Near Eastern prisons, but today the connection seems unavoidable. It is also noteworthy that as time has passed, Rowling's books seem to express a greater and greater suspicion of political authority. Nineteen years after the end of the series, not only Azekaban and the bumbling Ministry of Magic, but their Muggle equivalents, are still around.

Bad Husbands

Among the best-known fairy tales, "Bluebeard" is an oddity. Unlike "Snow White," "Cinderella," "Beauty and the Beast," and many others, it does not end with a marriage. "Bluebeard" is not even technically a fairy story: it contains no witches or fairy godmothers or magic transformations; there is only one minor supernatural element, the permanent stain of blood on the key to the forbidden chamber. Stories like "Cinderella" tell us that a troubled, often unhappy adolescence ends with a happy marriage; "Bluebeard" tells us that the real trouble begins after the wedding. In the classic tales, the prince is charming, but the heroine's relatives are either hostile or weak or both. In "Bluebeard," however, the husband has already killed several previous wives, and when the heroine discovers their bodies, he intends to murder her. She is rescued just in time, by her sister and brothers in some versions, her mother in others.

The heroine of this story is also, depending on how you

look at it, morally flawed or very unlucky or both. In the first printed version, as one of Charles Perrault's *Tales of Mother Goose* (1697), she initially finds Bluebeard hideously ugly. But after she and her family and friends spend a week at one of his luxurious country houses, where there are "dinner services of gold and silver, beautifully upholstered furniture, and carriages covered in gold leaf," she decides that his beard "was not really so blue after all," and agrees to marry him. Later, when he has given her the keys to every room in the house, but warned her to stay out of one small chamber, she can hardly wait to disobey his instructions.

As Maria Tatar says in *Secrets Beyond the Door: The Story of Bluebeard and His Wives*, the two most vital ingredients of the tale are "the curiosity of a woman and the secrets of a man." Though the moral at the end of Perrault's version warns against curiosity, several readers have remarked that the wife's inquisitiveness was justified, because she discovered that her husband was a serial killer. Tatar suggests that "our own culture has turned [Bluebeard's wife] into something of a heroine, a woman whose problem-solving skills and psychological finesse make her a shrewd detective, capable of rescuing herself and often her marriage."

"Bluebeard" is widely known: there are British, French, German, Italian, and Appalachian American versions, and the basic plot reappears in modern fiction, though often with a different ending or a different moral. In both Charlotte Brontë's *Jane Eyre* and Daphne du Maurier's *Rebecca*, for instance, the heroines, as Tatar puts it, "rather than aligning themselves with discovery and detection, become partners in crime," accessories after the fact. Going even further, she presents Nabokov's *Lolita* as a Bluebeard tale, one in which

Humbert Humbert destroys Lolita and her mother not by murdering them, but by writing about them.

One of the best and most original chapters in *Secrets Beyond the Door* deals with what Maria Tatar calls the "Bluebeard films" of the 1940s: films like George Cukor's *Gaslight* and Alfred Hitchcock's *Suspicion*, in which husbands who have large expensive houses and awful secrets try to kill their wives or drive them mad. In these films the wife gradually becomes strong and independent enough to uncover the secret, but she does not have a supportive family (often she is an orphan with no siblings) and she does not escape the marriage. As Tatar says, "The happy endings are, once again, a letdown. When the secrets beyond the door to marriage are solved, there is real closure. The woman who has passed beyond the door is now permanently encased behind it. . . . And this, above all else, becomes the real curse of living happily ever after."

Maria Tatar is also interesting on Bluebeard as a cultural hero, the victim rather than the villain of the story. In a chapter titled "Monstrous Wives" she traces a connection between modern fiction, drama, and film, and ancient views of women as insatiably and fatally curious, like the Biblical Eve and Lot's Wife, and the Greek Psyche and Pandora (who opened a forbidden chest and released every known evil into the world).

It is possible, of course, to read "Bluebeard" as a metaphor, a greatly exaggerated version of what marriage meant for many women in the past. In the seventeenth century, when Perrault first recorded the story, well-to-do and aristocratic women often married relative or even total strangers. In these marriages the bride was likely to be much younger

and less experienced than the groom. Exogamy was traditional: when the woman married she left home and moved
to wherever her husband lived and worked. Often she knew
no one there. A nice girl was also supposed to be a virgin on
her wedding day, while her husband was assumed to have
known other women. This was a pattern that persisted in
Europe well into the nineteenth and even the early twentieth
century.

Naturally, the new bride in such marriages was often
curious about her husband's past. Whom had he been
involved with before he met her? If he had rejected one or
more women, had there been violent, painful scenes? Was he
a "lady-killer" in the conventional sense? Was his symbolic
closet full of skeletons? Clues might appear in the form of
letters and photos, friends might gossip, and sometimes the
actual victims of the "lady-killer" would appear and tell their
unhappy stories to the current wife.

Speculating about the popularity of Bluebeard films in
the Hollywood of the 1940s, Maria Tatar points out that this
"was, after all, a time of crisis, when women in great numbers
were marrying men who were real strangers—soldiers going
off to war. . . . It was also a time when women were realizing
that the men to whom they had been married were becoming strangers. After experiencing the dark horrors of combat,
veterans returned home disaffected and alienated." Many of
these men had actually killed people—in a sense, like Bluebeard, they were murderers—and more often than not they
wanted to shut these events away in a locked cupboard of
their minds.

Today in America, it seems to me, the Bluebeard story
has a different sort of resonance. More than fifty percent of

marriages end in divorce, and most divorced people remarry; thus, many brides and grooms come to their wedding with important emotional baggage. Unpacking this baggage, especially by force, can be a big mistake. The story of Bluebeard may be relevant again now because it warns women against obsessive curiosity about their partner's past. The lesson is still delivered frequently, and now to both sexes; advice columnists warn their readers, both male and female, against revealing too much. They know that curiosity about this past can be destructive—even murderously destructive. Both women and men may discover that their spouses suffer from obsessive jealousy, not only spying on their daily life, but cross-questioning them about every date they have ever had. In this situation, "Bluebeard" still has meaning as a cautionary tale, warning us that though very few husbands or wives are serial killers, many have—and perhaps deserve to keep—their secrets.

Rapunzel: The Girl
in the Tower

At first glance most fairy tales seem so implausible and so irrelevant to contemporary life that their survival is hard to understand. The story of "Hansel and Gretel," for instance, asks us to believe that two children abandoned in a forest will soon find a house made of gingerbread. But these and other tales live on because they are dramatic metaphors of real life. "Hansel and Gretel," for instance, represents the two greatest fears of young children—that they will be abandoned, and that they will be imprisoned. Many adults, if they think back, will remember one or both of these fears, though usually in a less extreme version. Most of us occasionally felt neglected, disregarded, unsupported—unloved. Or we felt over-protected, over-indulged, intruded upon—loved, but in a very possessive, almost scary way.

The wicked stepmother who has no food for her children and the wicked witch whose house is made of cake and candy are dramatic, exaggerated images of two kinds of bad parent. They reappear symbolically in real life every Halloween, when the traditional warning "Never take candy from a stranger" is revoked; when we send our own children out into a dark world to forage for sweets, and stay home to give handfuls of foil-wrapped chocolates to kids we don't know.

Different features of a fairy tale may be important to different readers. When I taught children's literature, I discovered that for one of my students, "Hansel and Gretel" was essentially about a brave and clever girl who saves her brother from danger. For another, it was about a brave and clever boy who figures out how to find his and his sister's way home by marking their path through the woods. Later a friend told me that she had always thought of the tale as a warning against a greed for sweets.

"Rapunzel" was once much less widely known than "Hansel and Gretel." Currently, however, it has nearly three thousand entries on Amazon alone. Some of them are duplicates, but even the first hundred include fifty-one separate retellings, revisions, and spin-offs, including a pop-up book, a picture book starring Barbie as the heroine, mysteries, thrillers, romance novels, young adult fiction, and a pornographic S&M novel. There is a reason for this. "Rapunzel" is a complex story, which includes many classic themes, including a witch who is serially both kinds of bad parent: first imprisoning and then rejecting her foster daughter. It is also especially relevant today.

The earliest known appearance of the tale in print occurs in the *Pentamerone* by Giambattista Basile, published in Italy in 1637. His "Petrosinella," like the later and better-known version in Jacob and Wilhelm Grimm's *Household Tales*, begins with two intense cravings: that of a pregnant woman for a plant that grows in a garden next door, and that of a witch for a girl child. In Italy, Spain, and France, the plant the expectant mother longs for is parsley; in Grimm it is called "rapunzel." According to botanists, this is probably *Valerianella locusta*, known as *feldsaladt* in Germany, and in English as "corn salad" or "lamb's lettuce"; in other versions of the tale the plant is "rampion," *Campanula rapunculus*, known sometimes as *Rapunzel-Glockenblumen*.

An ancient and widespread folk belief proclaims that the food cravings of a mother-to-be must be satisfied; if they are not, she risks bad luck or a miscarriage. There may be scientific truth behind the superstition: possibly in these cases important nutrients are missing from the mother's diet. A poor woman who is pregnant in the wintertime, for instance, might lack vitamin C, folic acid, and iron, all abundant in dark-green vegetables, and one important characteristic of both parsley and lamb's lettuce is that they are resistant to frost.

Today, though between fifty and seventy-five percent of pregnant women in America report food cravings, a wish for salad greens is rare. Expectant mothers are more likely to crave fresh fruit, especially strawberries. A desire for chocolate or sweets is also common, and may suggest that the mother-to-be has previously denied herself sugar in order to remain fashionably thin. (On the Internet today it is possible to buy maternity T-shirts that read THE BABY WANTS CHOCOLATE, THE BABY WANTS ICE CREAM, or THE BABY WANTS STRAWBERRIES.) The medical disorder known as "pica," a hunger for nonfood substances, may occur in pregnancy as a compulsion to eat clay, plaster, toothpaste, or laundry starch; it has sometimes been explained as a need for calcium.

In the Grimms' tale the expectant mother grows pale, weak, and sickly; she tells her husband that if she cannot have the rapunzel that grows in the witch's garden, she will die. Responding to her desperation, he climbs the garden wall and steals the plant she craves. On a second visit the witch catches him; she allows him to take the greens, but only if he promises her the baby when it is born. In the *Pentamerone* it is the mother-to-be herself who steals parsley from the garden next door and has to give up her child, though not for several years. There is also a variant Italian tale, "Prunella," that leaves out the pregnancy: instead the poor child herself steals plums from a witch's tree, and is caught and imprisoned. From a nutritionist's point of view, she, too, perhaps, lacks vitamin C.

The heroine of all these stories has the same name as the plant, though sometimes in the diminutive form: Basile's heroine is called Petrosinella, and in French she is Persinette. Symbolically, the child replaces and becomes what has been stolen and eaten. (There is an echo here of the still current folk belief that whatever a woman craves during her pregnancy will later become her child's favorite food.) Popular experts on diet and cooking claim that we are what we eat, and it is not unusual for people to be called "Candy," "Honey," "Sugar," or "Peaches," both in real life and in fiction. (Though Judy Blume says that the names of her famous character, Fudge, and his little sister, Tootsie, were not consciously chosen for this reason, chocolate was for a long time her own favorite food.) More darkly, there is the implication that a child is a consumable commodity. As Maurice Sendak's Wild Things (who were, he has said, based on his own aunts and uncles) put it: "We'll eat you up, we love you so!"

To many readers the most memorable feature of "Rapunzel" is the incantation, "Rapunzel, Rapunzel, let down your hair," with its accompanying image of a beautiful young girl standing in the window of a tower with her incredibly long hair hanging down outside. At first, the witch who has adopted Rapunzel climbs up this hair to visit her, then a wandering prince does so with far-reaching consequences. Finally the witch hangs Rapunzel's chopped-off tresses from the window, and the prince, deceived, starts to climb them and then falls. He scratches his eyes out on the brambles that ring the tower, and becomes blind. If Rapunzel's hair had been of a normal length, none of this could have happened.

What is this about? Of course, for centuries almost all women in Europe and North America had what we would now consider very long hair, though it was not always visible. As Marina Warner points out in *From the Beast to the Blonde*, for many years loose hair was the sign of a virgin or unwedded girl, and thus stood for youth and innocence. After a woman married, she pinned her hair up and/or concealed it under some sort of cap or wrapping, except in private.

Long, thick hair has always been thought beautiful and erotically alluring: artists and writers have celebrated it as the sign of a lush, intensified womanliness. In nineteenth-century America it was a source of pride if you could actually sit on your hair, and to lose it was a disaster: when Jo in *Little Women* sells her thick chestnut mane, it is treated by her family as a kind of minor tragedy. Similarly, in "Rapunzel" and its variants the witch often begins her revenge by violently chopping off the heroine's hair.

The witch's, and later the prince's, demand that Rapunzel let down her hair echoes a colloquial phrase first recorded in print in the mid-nineteenth century, though it may be much older. To "let down one's hair" (or "let down one's back hair") still means to relax and drop one's reserve, to act or speak freely and unguardedly. This is what Rapunzel does, first when she accepts the prince as her lover, and then when she asks the witch why she is so much heavier to pull up than he is. (In the first and less bowdlerized edition of the Grimms' *Household Tales*, Rapunzel also asks why her dress is getting so tight, alerting the witch to a pregnancy that later results in twins.)

But though long, thick hair was often referred to as a "woman's glory," it was also her burden. Washing it, drying it, combing out the tangles, brushing it (fifty to a hundred strokes a day were recommended in ladies' magazines), plaiting it, pinning it up, and taking it down took a lot of time and effort. The brilliant children's writer E. Nesbit dramatized this problem in a 1908 fairy tale called "Melisande, or Long and Short Division," where the princess's golden hair grows so fast that she is almost immobilized. The date is significant, since in the early twentieth century many women could and did decide to wear their hair short. This choice, which now seems more or less inconsequential, was seen at the time as a serious, even dangerous sign of sexual freedom and independence. It was also often criticized as unattractive and unfeminine: F. Scott Fitzgerald's 1920 story "Bernice Bobs Her Hair" is a famous exploration of these issues.

In several modern versions of "Rapunzel" the heroine is oppressed by her magically elongated braid, which is so heavy and bulky that she can hardly move about her tower room. In the young-adult novel *Golden* by Cameron Dokey (2006), she exclaims, "You think *this* is beautiful?. . . You try living with it for a while. I trip over it when I walk. Get tangled up in it when I sleep. I can't cut it."

Another teenage novel, *Letters from Rapunzel*, by Sara Lewis Holmes (2007), takes a scientific approach to the problem of Rapunzel's hair. Here the first-person heroine is not really named after a plant; she adopts the pseudonym because she has to spend hours every day in study hall supervised by a teacher she calls The Homework Witch. Though she feels helpless and imprisoned, her essential problem is one of parental abandonment. Her father is also confined—hospitalized with depression (which she calls The Evil Spell) and her mother works long hours to support the family and spends most of her free time visiting her sick husband.

Having learned that human hair grows an average of six inches a year, the narrator calculates that the real Rapunzel must have been in her tower for eighteen years, which would make her thirty-one. For a junior high-school student this is an impossible age for romantic adventure, so she concludes that Rapunzel did not age in captivity. The lesson is clear: if you remain confined, you cannot grow up. Holmes's heroine doesn't just wait for a prince; instead, like the heroines of most young-adult novels, she eventually manages to rescue herself by taking responsibility for her own future.

Bruno Bettelheim remarks in his classic analysis of the fairy tale, *The Uses of Enchantment*, that "Rapunzel" is "the story of a pubertal girl, and of a jealous mother who tries to prevent her from gaining independence—a typical adolescent problem." But it can also be seen as a story about the adoption of a poor and beautiful young girl by a prosperous but over-possessive older woman, who later takes drastic but eventually unsuccessful measures to isolate her foster daughter from the world and especially from men. This plot, of course, also appears in adult literature. Charles Dickens's Miss Havisham, in *Great Expectations*, shuts her ward, Estella in a huge, decaying house and tries to teach her to hate all men. In Henry James's *The Bostonians*, Olive Chancellor essentially buys Verena Tarrant from her parents with greenbacks rather than green plants, takes her into her Boston mansion, and attempts to possess and control her life. In both cases the heroine eventually escapes, but only with great difficulty and not necessarily into a better life. (In none of the current versions of "Rapunzel" I have read is there any suggestion, as there is in *The Bostonians*—and even more strongly in Anne Sexton's poem "Rapunzel" and Emma Donoghue's *Kissing the Witch*—that the older woman is erotically interested in her ward. Instead, the problem is always maternal possessiveness.)

In the traditional tale of "Rapunzel" the character who trades garden produce for a poor neighbor's child is an unsympathetic figure. In Grimm she is called "Mother Gothel," which at the time was a common designation for a godmother, but she is not the sort of good fairy godmother who grants wishes. She is not actively unkind, however, until her daughter falls in love with a man. Mother Gothel considers this a betrayal, and becomes enraged, but the love affair is presented as innocent and natural, and the story ends with Rapunzel and her prince living happily ever after in his kingdom.

Contemporary versions of "Rapunzel" often have a different emphasis, and perhaps for a contemporary reason. Over the last few decades, more and more well-to-do Americans and Europeans have adopted the children of poor parents, often from third-world countries; and because of local cultural prejudices, most of these babies have been girls.

Generally, adoptive parents are treated in the media and

by friends and relatives, as good, kind, and generous. Many modern versions of "Rapunzel" take the same attitude. ("The witch was never unkind to Rapunzel. Indeed, she gave her almost everything the child could have wished for," says perhaps the best of these retellings, by Barbara Rogasky, beautifully illustrated by Trina Schart Hyman.) The witch's problem is that she not only wants to protect her child from the dangers of the world outside; she does not want the girl to grow up and leave her—fears and desires that many parents, perhaps particularly adoptive parents of only one child, will recognize. In the traditional story this natural wish takes a pathological form; yet in most versions the witch is not punished. As Bruno Bettelheim points out, her possessive love for Rapunzel is selfish and foolish, but not evil, and "since she acted from too much love for Rapunzel and not out of wickedness, no harm befalls her."

Several modern adaptations of "Rapunzel" for adolescents seem to function as cautionary tales. They offer support to girls who need to escape an over-possessive parent, but also express sympathy for the mother who has trouble letting her go. They encourage teenagers to seek independence without feeling guilty, and parents to accept the inevitable. *Zel* (1996), for instance, by the best-selling author Donna Jo Napoli, is a lively, dramatic retelling of "Rapunzel" as a historical novel. It is set in the remote sixteenth-century Swiss Alps, where magic and the almost total isolation of the heroine seem more believable. It expresses both sympathy for and criticism of the witch, who will give her beloved adopted daughter anything but freedom, and ends up almost driving her mad in near-solitary confinement. "She had to be tied to no one but me," the witch thinks. "Me, no one but me."

Of course, Zel eventually meets and falls in love with a young man. Meanwhile the witch, exhausted by her own possessiveness, by the spells necessary to maintain Zel's captivity in the tower, and by her own guilt, becomes a powerless ghost, able only to silently witness the traditional happy ending, which incidentally takes place in a warm semi-tropical country—the sort of country from which many adopted babies come today.

Some contemporary teenage versions of Rapunzel not only sympathize with the witch figure but also blame the original mother. Cameron Dokey's *Golden*, for instance, splits Rapunzel into two different young girls. One is born totally bald, rejected by her mother, and brought up on a remote farm by the loving small-time sorceress Melisande. The other, who has yards of golden hair, is Melisande's real daughter, who has been put into a state of suspended animation and imprisoned in a tower by a magician. The girls are more or less the same age, and can become friends and share adventures. Both end up with suitable husbands and remain close to Melisande. This story both excuses the guilt some adoptive parents may feel for depriving a mother of her child, and supports the search of grown children for their birth parents.

Adèle Geras's *The Tower Room* (1990) is a realistic modern version of Rapunzel, though one that eventually reverses its moral. It is the first volume of an engaging and well-written trilogy set in 1962 in a posh English girls' school, apparently based on Roedean (the alma mater of both Princess Diana and the sisters in Ian McEwan's *Atonement*), where Adèle Geras herself was a student and the exact contemporary of her heroine, Megan. The girls at "Egerton Hall" are cut off from the world, but life there is described affectionately and in fascinating detail. Megan's parents are dead; and her adoptive mother, Dorothy, a teacher at the school, is cool and distant rather than over-possessive. "In my heart," Megan writes, "I regard her as only a guardian and never think of her as a real mother. . . . She did try to be like a mother to me during the holidays, but it was as though she were copying maternal behavior she had seen in other people, and not quite succeeding."

As it turns out, Dorothy is in love with a young lab instructor called Simon, who hardly notices her. Instead he falls for Megan, climbs a convenient builder's scaffolding to her tower room, and seduces her. When Dorothy discovers the affair, she flies into a hysterical rage and orders them both to leave. Soon Megan finds herself living in a squalid studio flat near Gloucester Road tube station and working in a coffee bar, waiting long hours for Simon to return from a distant ill-paying job. It takes her only a couple of months to decide to leave him and return to Edgerton Hall and her two best friends (who are ingenious contemporary versions of Snow White and Sleeping Beauty), finish her last term, and go on to Oxford. In a sequel she is also happily reunited with Simon. The lesson seems to be that if you are denied real parental affection, you should resist the impulse to compensate by quitting school and running off with a young man, even if he is your true love.

The colorful and lavishly illustrated *Sugar Cane: A Caribbean Rapunzel*, by Patricia Storace (2007), is intended for children rather than adolescents, but it also includes a partially sympathetic witch figure, a sorceress called Madame Fate. Though everyone on the island fears her, she provides her adopted daughter, Sugar Cane, with a beautiful garden, a lovable pet monkey, and—an unusual innovation—a first-rate education:

> Since Madame Fate was a conjure-woman who could bring people back from the dead, all Sugar Cane's teachers were special. . . . Her guitar teacher was a five-hundred-year-old Gypsy from Spain, and her piano teacher a jazz master from New Orleans. An Arabian philosopher tutored her in mathematics. She learned poetry from a Greek epic poet, and storytelling from an African griot.

Sugar Cane, like the Grimms' version of the story, unites the lovers through music, when a young man hears the heroine singing in the tower. It also alters the traditional ending to include a happy musical reunion with both of Sugar Cane's original parents.

Not all modern versions of Rapunzel show sympathy with the witch, and a few of them penalize her, though not severely, at the end. This is true of Lynn Roberts's *Rapunzel*, a groovy fairy tale (2003), which appears to take place in New York in the 1970s. Both text and illustrations are very much of the period—cartoonish, way out, and upbeat. There is no pre-story involving any variety of lettuce: the heroine simply lives on the top floor of an apartment building with her mean Aunt Esme, who rides a motorcycle with the license plate EV1L. When Aunt Esme discovers her niece's friendship with a high-school rock musician, she forces her to climb down her own cut-off hair into what looks like a rather scary part of Manhattan. Rapunzel has to spend the night alone in a littered shop doorway, but she and her boyfriend and his band are soon happily united. Aunt Esme's only punishment is that without Rapunzel's hair as a kind of magical escalator she has to climb at least five flights of stairs to reach her apartment.

Barbie as Rapunzel (2002), which is based on a short Disney film, also features an unsympathetic adoptive parent. Again there is no prologue: we simply hear that the heroine is kept as a servant by "Gothel, a mean witch." The text reads as if it were made up by a six-year-old out of bits of fairy tales and Barbie-doll promotional material. Rapunzel is a rather blank character, but this may be the result of a deliberate choice on the part of the author or publisher. As a former Mattel Company executive, Ivy Ross, puts it:

> [Barbie] isn't anything in particular, so she becomes a vehicle for [girls'] dreams, their aspirations—their dress rehearsal for everyday life. Even when she's in a new movie, Barbie acts Rapunzel.

Barbie/Rapunzel, like most Disney heroines, has some embarrassingly cute animal companions—in this case a bunny rabbit and a fat little dragon with pink wings. Also, like all Barbies, she gets to try on different costumes, which presumably can be bought in the local Toys "R" Us. Eventually she goes to a ball, discovers her long-lost father (he is a king, making her a princess), and marries a prince who resembles Barbie's boyfriend, Ken. The witch ends up imprisoned in her own tower. In the view of some psychologists, the final reunion with only the father (which also occurs in many versions of "Hansel and Gretel") makes sense, either because it fulfills the daughter's unconscious desire to have him to herself, or because the witch is really the mother in disguise.

In the Grimms' tale of Rapunzel (though not in the *Pentamerone*), the prince is a fairly ineffective figure. After he

climbs Rapunzel's cut-off hair into the tower and is con-
fronted by the witch, he jumps from the window in despair
and is blinded by thorns. Both he and his beloved then wander about in misery for several years, but at last they find each
other, and when Rapunzel's tears fall on his eyes, his sight
is restored. In many modern versions the hero is a stronger
character. These stories usually omit his blinding, or treat it
metaphorically: he gets a concussion when he falls from the
tower, and cannot remember Rapunzel and his love for her;
or his glasses are broken and he can't see her, or he believes
that she has abandoned him rather than been banished to the
wilderness by the witch. In the end, however, the lovers are
reunited, one way or another. Men may appear to desert or
forget you, the moral seems to be, but not forever.

CLOTHES

Breaking the Laws of Fashion

For hundreds of years there were strict rules about what people could wear at different times of the day and year, and at different ages. At first actual laws limited certain colors and fabrics to aristocrats; later on, social custom rather than legal documents worked to enforce conformity. My father, for instance, always exchanged his gray felt hat for a pale yellow straw one when he left for work after breakfast on Memorial Day. When he got off the train that evening, he would be surrounded by dozens of other commuters in almost identical straw hats. After Labor Day, they all switched back to felt.

For women there were even more rules. In the 1960s, for instance, fashion magazines published illustrated guides to the proper length of the new miniskirt: "Grandmother's" hem ended just above the knee; "Mother's" three inches above the knee, and "Daughter's" six inches. During most of the twentieth century colors were sex-typed and age-typed from the cradle to the grave: light blue was favored for baby boys and pink for girls, and primary crayon colors were right for small children. When a little girl entered grade school, brown and tan and navy were added, and remained correct for the rest of her life. A woman with a white-collar job was supposed to wear dull, solid colors like navy blue and tan and white at work, perhaps with a brighter blouse or scarf. At home more variety was allowed, but for many years black was taboo before eighteen, and a married woman who wore a bright red evening dress after thirty might be seen as inviting scandal. Later, as she aged, she was supposed to abandon bright colors in favor of dimmed ones: gray and lavender were believed to be especially appropriate and becoming for old ladies.

Men, too, followed invisible social rules: boys wore green and blue and brown and tan and khaki, and their fathers more subdued versions of the same shades, plus gray. If you were in business, a gray, brown, or black suit, with a white shirt and a striped or small-patterned tie, was necessary, along with lace-up, highly polished shoes. In certain professions, and at certain times of year, the laws might be slightly relaxed to allow pale blue or tan shirts, and possibly even a blazer and slacks.

Outside the home, middle-class dress was formal and subdued. In the New York suburb where I grew up, a respectable woman did not use dramatic makeup during the day, or go out to lunch or into the city without gloves and a hat. If she had a white-collar job she wore a suit or a tailored dress and pumps. College students were expected to wear dresses and skirts to class; slacks were forbidden except in the coldest weather. Blue jeans and sneakers were fine for girls and women on vacation, but you could not wear them to a dinner party without suggesting that you disliked or scorned the host. The older you were, and the more formal the party, the worse the insult.

In the early and mid-twentieth century it was fairly easy to guess a woman's age. It wasn't just a matter of clothes: many middle-class American females stopped exercising seriously after they got married, though they might walk around a golf course once a week or play a couple of sets of tennis. Many women also had domestic help: they did not need to cook and wash and iron and mop and push a vacuum cleaner. As time passed, even if they didn't overeat, they gradually began to bulge in the wrong places, and their hair started to turn gray. There wasn't much they could safely do about it: most hair dyes created a glaringly fake effect, and some could be poisonous; plastic surgery was expensive, uncertain, and sometimes dangerous.

After World War II, however, all this changed. Now only the very rich had full-time domestic servants, and it was usually necessary to clean your own house and cook your own meals. It also became more and more fashionable to exercise. Medical advances meant that it was no longer obvious that someone had had a face lift. The rules about color also changed drastically. Bright colors were fine at any age, and both babies and grandmothers wore red.

For centuries, hair was an important indicator of a woman's age. Social custom required that young girls wore it long; after marriage it was covered with a cap or scarf, and/or confined in braids or a bun: in many societies custom still makes this obligatory. Even today, long hair, loose curls, and bangs all suggest youth; though if someone is under forty, a short stylish haircut can sometimes have the same effect, giving an adolescent gamine or tomboy look.

A woman over fifty who wears her hair very short will often be thought to have stopped caring about sex, especially if her clothes are drab and baggy. If her locks are long and flowing, she will be assumed to be interested, perhaps because the majority of men, according to report, prefer long hair; she may also be typed as either artistic or theatrical. But if she works in a business office, she may have a problem, since long, loose hair on the job is thought to indicate a lack of neatness and efficiency and attention to business, as well as inviting sexual harassment and decreasing your chance of promotion. Caught between the wish for professional success, and a natural desire to look attractive, many women find themselves perpetually seeking the perfect hairstyle, to the permanent advantage of beauty salons.

Of course, clothes not only have an effect on the observer: they also influence those who wear them. In jeans and a T-shirt and flat shoes a woman can run and dance like a schoolgirl. Heavy clothes that physically constrict her will make her move more slowly and awkwardly: she will not only look but feel older and less flexible. A woman of any age who is zipped and buttoned into a heavy tight jacket and skirt or slacks may walk and sit like a more mature and more conventional person than she really is. Some people will feel uncomfortable around her, expecting criticism; others may see her as sturdily powerful, and expect help. Soft, loose fabrics and soft colors will make her feel warm and comfortable, and encourage others to expect affection and sympathy.

Shoes are important. High heels make women taller, and sometimes cause them to feel more powerful, but they also limit impulsive movement, making it difficult or even painful to walk rapidly for any length of time, or climb stairs. After a while they will start to hurt a woman's feet, causing her to sit down at every opportunity. Then, if everyone else is standing, she will look and feel and possibly even act weaker and smaller. Since high heels also cause the hip-swinging unsteady gait that men are said to find sexy, they will encourage her to feel and act helpless, relying on charm rather than ability to get what she wants. Even worse, it may make it impossible for her to escape something that she definitely does not want. The old saying that clothes make the man is unfortunately even truer, sometimes dangerously so, for women.

Aprons

Wherever I live, an apron hangs on a hook in my kitchen. I use it to protect my clothes, wipe wet hands, lift hot lids, and pry open bottles of tomato juice or furniture polish that I suspect are planning to splash me with their contents. But without it, somehow, I can't cook as well. When I put it on, I am choosing a role and making a statement, and so is anyone else. Aprons, in all their many forms, are more than just protective devices; they are full of meaning.

There are many kinds of aprons, of course. My mother wore full calico aprons in old-fashioned flower patterns, with pockets and a square upper bib and ties that crossed in the back and fastened around the waist in front. Mine are half-aprons in bright rural colors: barn red, delphinium and sky blue, sunflower yellow. I usually make them myself out of leftover dress material or my husband's old shirts.

In the past most males never went near a stove unless they had to cook or starve, and most would almost rather starve than wear a woman's apron, even in private. (The sad, inept husband Dagwood, in the comic strip "Blondie," looked even more pathetic when he tied on one of his wife's aprons.) When I was a child, the only things my father would ever cook were popovers and Yorkshire pudding. Sometimes, when my mother had made a roast, he would come into the kitchen to demonstrate this skill. Before he began, he would awkwardly tuck a dishtowel into the band of his trousers.

This, of course, was before culinary activity became respectable for men who were not professional chefs. Back then, they were able to cook without embarrassment only if the activity were carefully decontaminated to make sure that there was nothing feminine about it. Men couldn't go into the kitchen, where getting dinner was easy and safe. They couldn't boil, bake, or sauté, or have anything to do with inexpensive dishes like salads or casseroles.

If men were going to cook, the process had to seem difficult and dangerous; it had to resemble the end of a caveman's successful big-game hunt. It had to take place outdoors, on a grill constructed of crude, masculine materials like rusty iron, smoke-smeared brick, and chunks of stone. It had to involve thick cuts of bloody meat and implements that suggested savage warfare: pitchforks and knives and griddles— and there had to be blazing flames, the more perilous-looking the better.

Of course, this kind of cooking was very messy. Since he wasn't wearing the caveman's costume of greasy animal skins, Dad's clothing had to be protected, but by something with as little as possible resemblance to a woman's apron. The solution was a garment that imitated medieval armor: a kind of extended breastplate made of heavy canvas or upholstery-strength plastic. These "barbecue aprons" are heavy, clumsy contraptions that fasten low around the hips and totally conceal the shape of the body beneath. The important thing about them is that they don't look sissy. To make sure that everyone gets the message, barbecue aprons are often printed with symbolically macho designs (meat-cutting diagrams, big game, sports cars) or slogans (BARBECUE BOSS, MASTER CHEF). Today, when women are allowed to use the outdoor grill, you can buy his and hers versions of this apron with similar legends.

There are, of course, some aprons that do not embarrass men, including the leather ones worn by woodworkers and other craftsmen, and the carpenters' aprons hung with tools. There are the aprons of grocery employees: the cashier's tie-on vests, the butchers' heavy-weight bloodied canvas, white or sometimes a light brown that helps to conceal the stains of dried blood. Gardeners may wear serious wrap-around aprons with high bibs and deep pockets for tools and seeds. As women took up these professions, they adopted the uniforms, or others like them: the light-weight gardening smock suitable for cutting flowers and bedding out plants, though not for serious digging, also suggests the working costume of a painter, and conveys the idea that gardening is an art form. Domestic cooks once always wore stiff, starched white aprons with high bibs and long straps that crossed in back; today they are mainly sold by firms that outfit servants and professional chefs.

All these costumes can also be seen on television shows, where their colors often vary according to the subject matter: TV gardeners favor green or tan aprons, suggesting leaves or earth, while TV cooks seem to prefer yellow and cream, suggesting butter and cheese, rather than the white of hired help, though Julia Child, who was supremely confident of her social status, used to wear a big white chef's apron on her TV show.

Waiters and waitresses, both in real life and on TV, wear aprons that are carefully chosen to express the ambiance of the establishment from the bright gingham ruffles of the ice-cream parlor to the discreet dark rectangles, heavy with pockets for tips, of the expensive restaurant. Both men and women who work in hairdressing prefer smocks, color-coordinated to the ambiance of the establishment—black for the serious high-end establishment, pink for the friendly local beauty salon. But though they often look stylish, these garments are also practical: spot-resistant, hair-shedding, washable, and well-equipped with pockets.

At the other extreme from all this is what might be called the imitation apron, which doesn't really protect its wearer from anything. Usually it is a kind of tiny, frilly creation of flounced silk or crisp ruffled cotton, with a big bow and sometimes flyaway streamers. These concoctions used to be known as "hostess aprons," and were often worn by women who had played no part in preparing a meal. In other cases, they signaled a switch of roles; when one of my mother's friends was cooking for a party, she would wear a big, practical bib apron; then, when guests were about to arrive, she would whip it off and put on a perfectly laundered and ironed miniature substitute. This wisp of cloth was not exactly a lie, because she really had made the dinner, but it suggested that she had done so effortlessly and without the slightest injury to her clothes.

Today, almost no hostess wears a hostess apron. If she did, it would be seen as a kind of camp gesture: a mock-assumption of old-fashioned femininity. Pretty, totally useless aprons are worn only by maids in French farces and soft-porn films, though they may perhaps be seen in the privacy of the home. If the separation of the sexes is seen as desirable and attractive, certain sorts of apron, not all completely useless from a practical point of view, may seem sexy. Back in the 1950s, one guide to pleasing and keeping a husband suggested that you meet him at the front door in the evening with his favorite alcoholic drink on a tray, wearing only high heels and a semi-transparent little apron. If a wife today were to try this trick, substituting her modern barbecue apron, the effect would be very different—though some might get away with it as a joke.

Like all clothes, aprons may have a symbolic as well as a practical function. To wear one over visible clothes allows you to say two things at once. The underlying getup makes a statement about who you are in "real life"; the apron announces that just for the moment you are also a cook, a gardener, or an artist, and it also says something about the value you assign to this temporary role. On TV cooking shows, not only are the aprons obviously carefully chosen and expensive, but expensive outfits are often visible underneath, to remind us that the presenter is not a servant but a highly paid professional performer.

Recently a friend told me that she never wears an apron; she just wraps "some old rag" around her waist. Is she saying that, for her, cooking is a ratty, unpleasant job? And, if so, would it really be a good idea to go to her house for dinner?

The Mystery of Knitting

K nitting is a kind of domestic magic. I first suspected this as a child when I watched my mother turn a one-dimensional substance—a long red woolen string—into two and finally three dimensions: a stocking cap for my doll, with shape and weight, an inside and an outside. Appropriately, this transformation was accomplished with long shiny sticks, like the magic wands, in fairy stories. And it wasn't only the materials that, for me, were transformed. The women who could perform this magic were, in everyday life, everyday humans; but when they picked up their wands they became practitioners of a secret art. The same thing happened in my books. In "The Six Swans," from the Grimms' *Household Tales*, for instance, six princes are changed into birds by their wicked stepmother. Their sister can break the spell by knitting magical shirts for them out of flowers; she does not quite finish in time, however, and the youngest brother returns to human shape with a swan's wing instead of his left arm.

Of course, this folktale can be read as a kind of allegory. Women have attempted for hundreds of years to transform wild, free-ranging men into affectionate domestic creatures with the help of hand-made garments, and have sometimes succeeded. Popular culture and advertising have kept the idea alive. "He'll love you more if you knit for him!" cried a yarn manufacturer in the 1950s, and *Seventeen* magazine, calling up a rather spooky image, twittered, "You can knit that man right out of your life or—better advice—you can knit one right in."

My mother, like most of her friends, knew how to knit, but she preferred sewing, and made charming clothes for my and my sister's dolls on her old Singer treadle sewing machine. When I was seven, she tried to teach me how to knit, but without success. Under her reluctant instruction I managed about twelve inches of a lumpy scarf in alternating wobbly stripes of ugly brown and canary-yellow wool. Then I gave up, and for several years refused to try again.

My mother was of Scottish descent, and always unwilling to waste anything. She took over the wool and created an afghan of alternating brown and yellow squares. It lasted a long time, and was loved by my younger sister and eventually by both her children and mine. For one of them it temporarily became a beloved and comforting "blankie," or, as psychologists call it, a "transitional object."

Eventually a friend of my mother's managed to teach me to knit in the rapid European method, in which the yarn is held in the left hand and there is less movement of the arms. My first project was also a scarf, but this time a more successful one, in a soft blue wool.

Of the domestic handicrafts, knitting is both the most

magical and the simplest. It is also probably very old. Few
ancient examples have survived, though some socks from
Egypt are believed to date from the eleventh century. Archae-
ologists have found many more woven than knitted textiles,
but it seems likely that knitting and crocheting pre-date
weaving. Weaving, after all, demands a settled environment
and bulky equipment in the form of a loom. Knitting requires
little in the way of equipment and can be carried about from
place to place and combined with other tasks such as homework or watching small children. It does not demand strong
light or a steady hand, and would therefore be well suited to
nomadic people who followed the migrations of game or the
seasonal ripening of fruits, vegetables, and nuts.

By the late Middle Ages knitting was well-established,
and widespread. A fourteenth-century painting by Bertram
von Minden shows the Virgin Mary finishing up what looks
like a small pink short-sleeved top, presumably for her young
son. Weavers and seamstresses worked sitting down, but it is
possible to knit while standing, or even while walking. You
can do it when it is too dark to sew, something that was especially important before the invention of electricity. Knitting
wasn't just a hobby, as it often is today, but an essential household craft. Either you made socks, scarves, and sweaters for
yourselves and your family, or you went without. Shepherds
and shepherdesses traditionally knit as they watched their
flocks, and there are many seventeenth-, eighteenth-, and
early nineteenth-century paintings of women in peasant dress
knitting, often while standing up.

Since it did not demand physical strength, knitting was
something you could do at any age, and to judge by the art
of the period, the very young and the very old were frequent

knitters. Some not only supplied their families but made goods for sale, including fine silk stockings for the rich. *Young Knitter Asleep*, by the eighteenth-century French artist Jean-Baptiste Greuze, shows a little girl six or seven years old who has dozed off over this monotonous task.

Crochet, patterns for which first appeared in the early nineteenth century, was at first a very different kind of hand-icraft. It belonged to what was often called "fancywork," which included tatting, tapestry, and embroidery. The important thing about fancywork was that it was both artistic and unnecessary. It was the leisure occupation of well-to-do women who did not have to create anything essential. Instead they demonstrated their taste and skill by making decorative objects: embroidered handkerchiefs and slippers, lace for edgings and trimmings, little net purses, doilies and runners for tables, and antimacassars for sofas and chairs. Knitting was practical and plebian; fancywork was prestigiously use-less and ladylike.

In nineteenth-century fiction, very often, good women knit and bad women do fancywork. In Jane Austen's *Emma*, the long-suffering good girl, Jane Fairfax, is a dedicated knitter, as is her aunt, Miss Bates. Emma herself does not knit. Hester in Nathaniel Hawthorne's *The Scarlet Letter* is a self-supporting single mother who knits and sews for a liv-ing. In *Vanity Fair,* Thackeray's anti-heroine, Becky Sharp, practices fine "netting" in order to show off her long white fingers and catch her chosen fish, Josiah Smedley.

In Tolstoy's *Anna Karenina*, Levin's loyal and lovable wife, Kitty, knits while she is in labor with her first child. Anna her-self, on the other hand, crochets nervously as she confronts her love, Count Vronsky, who has just returned from a party:

"You don't know what I have suffered waiting for you [she says]. I believe
I'm not jealous. I'm not jealous. I believe you when you're here; but when
you're away somewhere leading your life, so incomprehensible to me...."
She turned away from him, pulled the hook at last out of the crochet
work, and rapidly, with the help of her forefinger, began working loop
after loop of the wool that was dazzlingly white in the lamplight, while
the slender wrist moved swiftly, nervously in the embroidered cuff.

American domestic history took place to the accompa-
niment of the steady clicking of thousands of needles and
crochet hooks: wood, bone, steel, and plastic. Pioneer women
report knitting by firelight and on the swaying seats of covered wagons, and knitters still often carry their work with
them: even today you will see them at work on long plane or
train journeys. From the Colonial period on, directions for
knitting projects in newspapers and magazines followed current trends. The practical shawls and heavy wool socks of the
early settlers and Western pioneers were supplemented in the
Victorian era by fluffy, light-weight wraps and lacy scarves
with names like "The Cloud" and "The Fascinator."

In the 1920s, daring flappers made themselves little cloche
hats and "hug-me-tight" sweaters; during the Depression
and World War II, there was a fashion for dark knitted wool
dresses and suits which resembled a kind of protective armor
against the (often literally) cold world. After the war, knitting
became softer and lighter again, and directions for clothing
the baby boom were everywhere: it was now possible, and
fashionable, to knit a complete layette, plus sweaters with
Scandinavian designs, for your husband and older children.
In the counterculture 60s and 70s, knitting became a quick,
cheap way to look cool and young: directions for creating

big loose-fringed shawls and multicolored vests and afghans in flower patterns were everywhere: I and my friends made many of them.

Whenever there was a war, though, knitting became virtuous and practical as well as, or instead of, decorative. At intervals over the last three hundred years, thousands of American women attached themselves to balls of navy-blue, gray, and khaki yarn, and as the *New York Times* put it, "Armies Marched on Hand-Knit Socks." In Louisa May Alcott's *Little Women,* both Jo and Beth knit for the troops. Beth knits happily and uncomplainingly, though when her father's letter from camp is read aloud, she becomes weepy and pauses. But then "she wiped away her tears with the long blue army sock, and began to knit again with all her might." Jo's reaction is different.

> "It's bad enough to be a girl, anyway [she says], when I like boy's games and work and manners. I can't get over my disappointment in not being a boy. And it's worse than ever now, for I'm dying to go and fight with Papa. and I can only stay home and knit, like a poky old woman!" And Jo shook the blue army sock till the needles rattled like castanets, and her ball bounded across the room.

The tradition of patriotic knitting continued for years. During World War I, President Wilson marched down Fifth Avenue ahead of a six-mile-long procession of Red Cross workers, some of them beating on tin buckets with knitting needles, and others carrying poles adorned with hand-knit military socks, now khaki instead of blue. In the last years of World War II, when I and my friends were in college, we were recruited as knitters, and met weekly in a Unitarian

Church in Cambridge. I still remember the hanks of heavy, slightly oily khaki yarn we were issued, and the blurred greenish mimeographed patterns for scarves and socks. The more expert knitters among us were also able to produce thick gloves, and mud-colored khaki helmets that covered the entire head and neck except for eye- and mouth-holes, a style now seen mostly on skiers and people who hold up drugstores. When I arrived on my first day as a volunteer and was met by a figure wearing one of these death's-heads, I was for a moment terrified.

In fact, this apparition should have been no surprise; the association between knitting and death is a persistent one. Readers of Joseph Conrad's *Heart of Darkness* will remember the two women, one young and one old, who sit silently knitting black wool in the office of the company that is about to send his hero Marlowe to the Congo. As Marlowe looks at the older of the two, he tells us:

> An eerie feeling came over me. She seemed uncanny and fateful. Often far away there I thought of these two, guarding the door of Darkness, knitting black wool as for a warm pall, one introducing continually to the unknown, the other scrutinizing the cheery and foolish faces with unconcerned old eyes. Ave! Old knitter of black wool, Morituri te salutant. Not many of those she looked at ever saw her again—not half, by a long way.

The most famous and sinister wartime knitter in literature, of course, is Dickens's Madame Defarge in A *Tale of Two Cities*, set in Paris at the time of the French Revolution. Madame Defarge, whose husband keeps a wine shop, is a tall, handsome, black-haired woman in her forties. Her father, brother, and sister have died as the result of the cruelties of an aristocrat, and she seeks revenge on him and his family. As she waits for them to be condemned to the guillotine, she goes every day to watch the executions, knitting the names of victims into her work. Dickens did not wholly invent this story; scholars tells us that revolutionary women would often knit as they stood watching public executions.

The best-known knitter in twentieth-century fiction is also closely associated with violent death, though as a benevolent rather than a malevolent character. This is Agatha Christie's Miss Marple, an elderly lady and amateur detective who lives in a tiny English village, where she solves one crime after another. Anyone who has spent time in such a village, or cast even the most passing glance at statistics, cannot help but be surprised at the number of murders that take place in or near St. Mary Mead. Can it be that Miss Marple's hobby somehow draws victims there? After all, there has always been an uncanny aspect to knitting, sometimes good, as with my mother's afghan, and sometimes not. A steel needle can be a weapon, especially if the point has been quietly sharpened. There are several instances of murder by knitting needle in detective fiction, but as far as I know, no character has ever been killed with a crochet hook.

Even in real life, many knitters are aware of the supernatural side of their craft. What is widely known among us as "the sweater curse" is recognized as a superstition, but it is one which some personal accounts support. Essentially it says that if you start knitting a sweater for any man in whom you have a serious romantic interest, you will break up before it is finished. One knitter I know claims that it also happens with scarves.

The rational explanation for the curse is that a handmade

sweater is typically thick, elastic, and clingy; it suggests to a man that the woman who is knitting it wants to surround and enclose him. To be presented with such a garment is a signal that its maker has serious plans for his future. If he is not ready for this, the gift may embarrass him and frighten him away. (The same phenomenon, according to some informants, has been observed in a relationship between two women.) It has been claimed that knitting a deliberate mistake into the sweater will break the curse, but my friends say that this doesn't always work. As a result, knitters are usually advised to wait until after the wedding to start any such project—especially since many also believe that a sweater made for a husband both keeps him safe and warm at home and wards off other women.

Zippers

Zip! I was reading Schopenhauer last night,
Zip! And I think that Schopenhauer was right . . .
Zip! I'm an intellectual.
                        —Lorenz Hart: "Zip!" from *Pal Joey*

The zipper is probably the only clothes fastener ever to
have been the star of a Broadway show tune. When Pal
Joey's highbrow striptease artist, based on Gypsy Rose Lee,
shed bits of her spangled costume, she demonstrated the zipper's amazing properties, of which the most remarkable is
speed.

The zipper revolutionized not only dressing, but undress-
ing—and in the process changed relations between the sexes.
For centuries, getting your clothes off and on was a slow and
often an awkward process, and one that you could not always
manage on your own. It was also precarious: hooks came
undone, drawstrings and laces knotted or broke, pins made

holes in you and in the fabric, buttons popped, and button-holes tore.

For years getting dressed took most middle- and upper-class people a long time, while getting undressed could take so long that it might be dangerous. In the Middle Ages knights sometimes bled to death on the battlefield before they could be unbuckled and unhooked from their tin-can armor. In the eighteenth and nineteenth centuries a lady's formal gown might have twenty or thirty buttons, and underneath these gowns fashionable women were often laced into corsets that made it impossible for them to take a deep breath. They sometimes fainted from exertion, and might even suffer permanent damage before they were freed.

The creation of the zipper was a slow process. The original "clasp locker" exhibited by Whitcomb L. Judson at the 1893 World's Fair in Chicago was clumsy and bulky. Many inventors, some of them women, worked to improve it. Finally, in 1917, Gideon Sundback patented the device we know today. In World War I, his "hookless fasteners" appeared on life-vests and flying suits for the Army and Navy; and B. F. Goodrich, who gave the device its name, put it on galoshes in the 1920s. But it wasn't until the mid-1930s that zippers were light and flexible enough to be used on fashionable clothing.

At first these zippers, always of metal, were usually concealed by flaps of fabric, though they were occasionally visible on military uniforms in World War II. But it was not until the 1960s that they really came out into the open. Suddenly bright-colored, often supersized zippers began to run up the front of stiff synthetic or cotton pique mini-dresses, and matching shiny boots, making women look as if they were wearing the covers of small kitchen appliances.

The other post-war apotheosis of the zipper was the biker look. Marlon Brando set the style in *The Wild Ones*, and even today black-leather motorcycle jackets still bristle with shiny, sharp-tabbed metal zippers that suggest not only secrecy (all those little pockets and pouches) but speed and violence—and also often sex.

But, as a film expert I know says, "When you're talking about zippers, you're already talking about sex." A dress that fastens with a long row of little buttons is a romantic challenge. A man needs patience, dexterity, and persuasive charm to get you out of it. A visible zipper, especially if it is partially unfastened, is a sort of silent come-on, but the kind of sex it suggests is passionate and immediate rather than romantic and long-term. Peeling your girlfriend (or your boyfriend) like a banana appears to be, and sometimes actually is, the work of a moment.

Life After Fashion

Soon after I reached sixty, I was abandoned by *Vogue* magazine and all its clones. Like former lovers who drop you slowly and politely, because they once cared for you, they gradually stopped speaking to me. Without intending it, I had permanently alienated them, simply by becoming old. From their point of view, I was now a hopeless case. They were not going to show me any more pictures of clothes I might look good in, or give me useful advice about makeup or hair.

At first, my feelings were hurt. Hadn't I loved Fashion and been faithful to her all these years? Just as one avoids the songs that recall a lost lover, I stopped reading her magazines, even in a doctor's office. As a result, I felt first panic and then, with surprise, a rush of euphoria. I was abandoned and alone, yes, but I was also free: after nearly half a century, nobody was telling me what to wear.

Since Fashion no longer pursued and flattered and

scolded me, I realized that I did not have to pursue her. I could go through my closet and get rid of all the stylish clothes I really didn't like: the little fitted jackets, the cropped pants that left six inches of pale stubbled leg hanging out, the silk dress-for-success blouses with floppy bows and padded shoulders. I also gave away everything too obviously "sexy"— that is, shiny and low-cut and tight and uncomfortable. I hadn't worn these outfits for years, essentially because I didn't want to look as if I were hopelessly trying to inflame passion in members of the opposite sex.

What was even better was that I could revive clothes I had loved in the past and hadn't been able to bear to throw away, though they had become completely out of date. The long patchwork hippie skirts and vests, the filmy scarves and big soft shawls, the loose cowl-neck sweaters, the floppy straw hats, some with feathers or artificial flowers. Some of these things were so far out of date that they looked new, and if they didn't, I didn't care.

Next I got rid of all my high-heeled shoes. I hadn't worn them very often since I slipped on an outdoor stairway covered with wet leaves and broke my leg. I had already understood that if I had been wearing flat shoes that day, I would have avoided a miserable week in the hospital and three months on crutches. Some of these shoes were beautiful in themselves, and giving them away was hard. But it was also a relief, because though fashion magazines don't admit it, high heels always slow you down and hurt your feet. (Whenever you are in a restaurant, you can see that under the partial cover of the tablecloths at least half the women there have taken off their painful spike-heeled pumps and sandals, just as my friends and I used to do.) Fashion pretends to be a feminist, but she still makes it almost impossible for anyone under her spell to negotiate a subway grating or a rough gravel path, or run for a bus without turning her ankle.

After a while, since Fashion was no longer nagging me to color my hair, I stopped, and in a few weeks it was almost white. This led to a wonderful discovery. For over sixty years I had been a brownish blonde, first naturally and then artificially, and half the spectrum had been out of bounds. Yellow and orange and coral and pink made my hair seem dirty as well as "dirty-blonde"; purple and lavender made me look like an Easter-egg basket full of dried straw. Now all this was over. White and gray hair go well with every color, including white and gray. It is no coincidence that some feminists have adopted as a slogan the first line of a poem by Jenny Joseph: "When I am an old woman I shall wear purple."

Already I had saved the two hours a month I had spent trying to turn my hair into a dull imitation of its original color and then cleaning up the mess in the sink afterwards. Next, with my husband's encouragement, I saved more time by throwing away my makeup. Powder and foundation and eye-shadow tend to cake in wrinkles, and an aging woman with bright-red lipstick, especially when it has leaked into the little, otherwise invisible lines around her lips, can look like an elderly vampire, or worse. She can become the sort of terrifying figure that the Ancient Mariner saw on the death-ship:

> Her lips were red, her looks were free,
> Her locks were yellow as gold . . .
> The Nightmare LIFE-IN-DEATH was she,
> Who thicks man's blood with cold . . .

Some of my friends made similar changes, all individual and all in defiance of Fashion. One gave away all her skirts and went into pants and jeans for the duration; another disobeyed the rule that dresses are now for formal occasions only and began sewing herself loose-cut casual smocks and muumuus in an unfashionable mid-calf length: she is a serious gardener, and points out that it is much easier to wash your knees than to wash a pair of slacks. Another friend decided that she would simplify her basic wardrobe to basic black, with accents of purple or green or scarlet.

All of us realized with joy that we could now wear whatever clothes we liked best. There was only one rule: we had to be reasonably neat. It may be true that, as the poet Robert Herrick put it, "a sweet disorder in the dress / Kindles in youth a wantonness," but in old age what it kindles is the suspicion that you are starting to lose your mind. Spiky, confused-looking hair of the sort that goes to fashionable clubs, ragged hems, torn-up jeans, and unraveling sweaters no longer look appealing. Realizing this, even the most charmingly untidy of my friends have now reformed. We do still see some unfortunate contemporaries who haven't learned this rule—and also, alas, some who are still worshipping at the altar of Fashion, who has forever turned her back on them.

ABOUT THE AUTHOR

Alison Lurie, who won the Pulitzer Prize for her novel *Foreign Affairs*, has published ten books of fiction, four works of nonfiction, and three collections of tales for children. She is a professor emerita of English at Cornell University, and lives in upstate New York with her husband, the writer Edward Hower.

PERMISSIONS

The lines from James Merrill's "Prose of Departure" appear courtesy of the literary estate of James Merrill © The Literary Estate of James Merrill.

The use of material from the works and letters of Edward Gorey are used by permission of the Edward Gorey Charitable Trust.